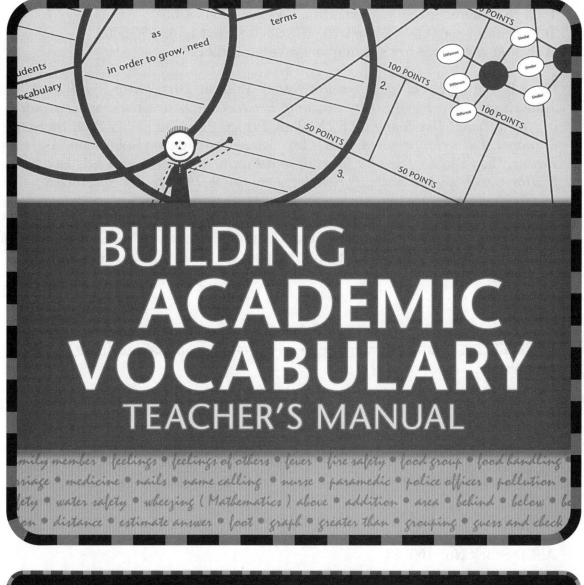

# BUILDING ACADEMIC VOCABULARY
## TEACHER'S MANUAL

## Robert J. Marzano • Debra J. Pickering

**Association for Supervision and Curriculum Development**
Alexandria, Virginia USA

Association for Supervision and Curriculum Development
1703 N. Beauregard St. • Alexandria, VA 22311-1714 USA
Telephone: 1-800-933-2723 or 1-703-578-9600 • Fax: 1-703-575-5400
Web site: www.ascd.org • E-mail: member@ascd.org

Gene R. Carter, *Executive Director*; Nancy Modrak, *Director of Publishing*;
Julie Houtz, *Director of Book Editing & Production*; Sally Chapman, *Director
of New Product Development*; Rick Allen, *Project Manager*; Mary Beth Nielsen,
*Manager, Editorial Services*; Kim Pifer, *Copyeditor*; Joanna Robertson, *Assistant
Editor*; Gary Bloom, *Director, Design and Production Services*; Chris Duncan,
*Senior Designer*; Jim Beals, *Typesetter*; Eric Coyle, *Production Specialist*.

ASCD is a community of educators, advocating sound policies and sharing best
practices to achieve the success of each learner. Founded in 1943, ASCD is a nonpartisan education association with headquarters in Alexandria, Virginia, USA.

ASCD publications present a variety of viewpoints. The views expressed or
implied in this manual should not be interpreted as official positions of the
Association.

Printed in the United States of America

ASCD Stock No.: 105153

ISBN No.: 1-4166-0234-8

ASCD member price: $19.95    nonmember price: $25.95

10   09   08   07   06   05          10   9   8   7   6   5   4   3   2

# BUILDING ACADEMIC VOCABULARY TEACHER'S MANUAL

## Contents

*For easier classroom reference, Appendix B has been numbered to correspond with the *Building Academic Vocabulary: Student Notebook* word lists.

# 1 | The Need for a Program to Build Academic Vocabulary

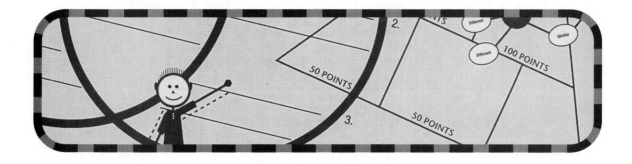

This manual will enable you to design and implement a comprehensive approach to teaching academic vocabulary as a district, a school, or an individual classroom teacher. The rationale for and research behind this approach are described in depth in *Building Background Knowledge for Academic Achievement: Research on What Works in Schools* (Marzano, 2004). We strongly encourage you to read it.

Teaching specific terms in a specific way is probably the strongest action a teacher can take to ensure that students have the academic background knowledge they need to understand the content they will encounter in school. When all the teachers in a school focus on the same academic vocabulary and teach it in the same way, the school has a powerful comprehensive approach. When all the teachers in a district embrace and use the approach, it becomes even more powerful.

To illustrate the effect of a systematic approach to teaching academic vocabulary, let's consider some of the research presented in *Building Background Knowledge for Academic Achievement*. Figure 1.1, for example, depicts two situations.

The bar on the left-hand side of the figure depicts a student who is at the 50th percentile in terms of ability to comprehend the subject matter taught in school,

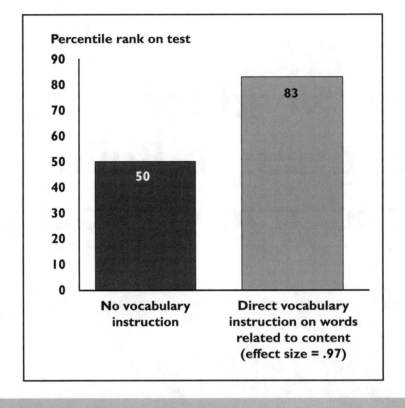

Figure 1.1 | **Impact of Direct Vocabulary Instruction**

with no direct vocabulary instruction. The bar on the right-hand side shows the comprehension level of the same student after specific content-area terms have been taught in a specific way. As you can see, the student's comprehension ability has increased to the 83rd percentile. This dramatic increase provides a strong argument for teaching academic terms.

Why, you might ask, does vocabulary instruction have such a profound effect on student comprehension of academic content? The answer to this question is straightforward. People's knowledge of any topic is encapsulated in the terms they know that are relevant to the topic. For example, people who know a great deal about snow skiing understand terms such as *fall line, snow plow, corn snow, unweight, powder, packed powder, green slope, blue slope, black slope, mogul, carving, and face-plant.* Likewise, students who understand the content in their state mathematics standards document regarding data analysis and statistics have an understanding of terms such as *mean, median, mode, range, standard deviation, and central tendency.*

The more students understand these terms, the easier it is for them to understand information they may read or hear about the topic. On the other hand, without a basic knowledge of these terms, students will have difficulty understanding information they read or hear.

Knowledge of important terms is critical to understanding any subject. If, for example, you are a snow skier, the following advice from a ski instructor is easy to understand. If you are not a snow skier, it probably makes little sense.

> Carving is appropriate for most green and blue slopes and even some black slopes. However, if you try to carve through moguls, especially in packed powder or corn snow, you're going to face-plant.

Although a bit contrived, this illustration makes the point that the more terms a person knows about a given subject, the easier it is to understand—and learn—new information related to that subject. This general knowledge is referred to as background knowledge. When students have general knowledge of the terms that are important to content taught in school, they can be said to have the necessary academic background knowledge.

Many students acquire academic background knowledge outside of school and come to subject-area classes already knowing and using terms essential for understanding content. For example, they or their families may have traveled extensively, exposing them to a variety of individuals, experiences, and cultures. Such students commonly take part in conversations at home that involve abundant information that will be useful to them in school. In short, they may have quite incidentally gained the academic background knowledge they need to succeed in school. By contrast, students from families with fewer resources may have lacked such opportunities and, thus, have not incidentally acquired important academic background knowledge.

These two types of students—those from academically advantaged environments and those from academically disadvantaged environments—enter school with significant discrepancies in terms of their chances for academic success. Unfortunately, as time progresses, the gap in academic background knowledge grows even larger, as does the gap in academic achievement between the two groups.

Given the importance of academic background knowledge and the fact that vocabulary is such an essential aspect of it, one of the most crucial services that teachers can provide, particularly for students who do not come from academically advantaged backgrounds, is **systematic instruction in important academic terms.**

This manual describes the specifics of such an approach and contains a list of 7,923 terms across 11 subject areas. Following the suggestions in this manual, an individual teacher, a school, or an entire district can design and implement a comprehensive program to teach and reinforce academic terms and, consequently, greatly enhance students' chances of learning the academic content presented in subject matter classes.

# References

Marzano, Robert J. (2004). *Building background knowledge for academic achievement: Research on what works in schools.* Alexandria, VA: Association for Supervision and Curriculum Development.

Stahl, S. A., & Fairbanks, M. M. (1986). The effects of vocabulary instruction: A model-based meta-analysis. *Review of Educational Research, 56*(1), 72–110.

# 2 | Creating a List of Academic Vocabulary Terms

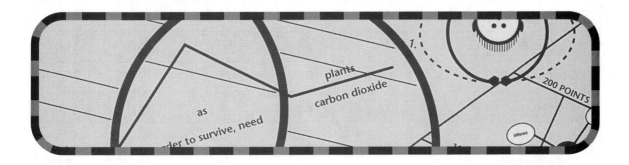

Appendix B of this manual lists 7,923 terms drawn from 11 subject areas. As *Building Background Knowledge for Academic Achievement* describes, these terms were extracted from national standards documents. In general, for each subject area, the terms are organized into four grade-level intervals: K–2, 3–5, 6–8, and 9–12. Figure 2.1 shows the number of terms in each subject area for each interval.

Of course, all 7,923 terms cannot be directly taught—nor should they be. Not enough time exists in the school day or year to do so. And even if there *were* enough time to devote to such an endeavor, it would not be advisable, because not all of the listed terms are *critically* important for all students to know.

Although the terms were drawn from national standards documents, some might not be found in your state-level standards documents. Additionally, not all terms (even if found in your state standards documents) are of equal importance. Some are *critically* important to the understanding of a given subject area, others are *useful but not critical,* and still others are *interesting but not very useful.* The list in Appendix B does not make such distinctions, because decisions about what is important should be made at the school or district level.

| Subject Area | Level 1 (K–2) | Level 2 (3–5) | Level 3 (6–8) | Level 4 (9–12) | Totals |
|---|---|---|---|---|---|
| Mathematics | 80 | 190 | 201 | 214 | 685 |
| Science | 100 | 166 | 225 | 282 | 773 |
| English Language Arts | 83 | 245 | 247 | 223 | 798 |
| History | | | | | |
| General History | 162 | 560 | 319 | 270 | 1,311 |
| U.S. History | 0 | 154 | 123 | 148 | 425 |
| World History | 0 | 245 | 301 | 297 | 843 |
| Geography | 89 | 212 | 258 | 300 | 859 |
| Civics | 45 | 145 | 210 | 213 | 613 |
| Economics | 29 | 68 | 89 | 155 | 341 |
| Health | 60 | 68 | 75 | 77 | 280 |
| Physical Education | 57 | 100 | 50 | 34 | 241 |
| The Arts | | | | | |
| General Arts | 14 | 36 | 30 | 9 | 89 |
| Dance | 18 | 24 | 42 | 37 | 121 |
| Music | 14 | 83 | 67 | 32 | 196 |
| Theater | 5 | 14 | 35 | 13 | 67 |
| Visual Arts | 3 | 41 | 24 | 8 | 76 |
| Technology | 23 | 47 | 56 | 79 | 205 |
| **TOTALS** | **782** | **2,398** | **2,352** | **2,391** | **7,923** |

Figure 2.1 | **Number of Terms Per Level in Each Subject Area**

Using the list in the Appendix as a resource, a district or school can create a list of a *few* terms from specific content areas that are so important to the understanding of those content areas that the district or school wants to guarantee they are taught to all students. This simple but powerful action can ensure that all students are exposed to information that will help them master important academic content. However, individual teachers working in isolation can also use the list to design a vocabulary program for their students. We begin with a discussion of this scenario.

# When Teachers Choose the Terms

If you are an individual classroom teacher working in isolation to create a comprehensive program, the terms listed in Appendix B can be a valuable resource. Here we will consider two situations: (1) a teacher responsible for a number of subjects within a self-contained classroom, and (2) a teacher responsible for teaching a single subject to a number of classes.

## Teaching in a Self-Contained Classroom

Typically, if you are a teacher in a self-contained classroom at the elementary level, you meet with the same students throughout the day and teach most, if not all, academic subjects. Let's assume, for purposes of illustration, that you are a 4th grade teacher in a self-contained classroom and that you are responsible for teaching language arts, mathematics, science, and social studies. To construct a list of academic vocabulary terms for your class, first determine a reasonable number of terms to teach throughout the school year—for example, one new term in each subject area each week, for 30 of the 36 weeks of school. This would mean teaching 4 new terms per week for 30 weeks, for a total of 120 terms taught across four subject areas during the school year. Note that your first estimates of the number of terms that you will teach are just that—estimates—and you can change them as you find necessary during the remaining planning stages of your program.

Next, consult Appendix B of this manual to examine the Level 2 terms (i.e., terms for grades 3–5) for language arts, mathematics, and science. Social studies is a hybrid subject area that cuts across general history, U.S. history, world history, geography, civics, and economics. Of these, general history probably contains most of the terms considered important to 4th grade social studies, but, to be thorough, you should examine the terms in all the social studies areas.

Of course, the lists for each subject area contain many more terms than you will teach. To select the 30 mathematics terms for the program you've designed, use the following question as your criterion: Is this term critically important to the mathematics content I will be teaching this year? As you scan through the Level 2 terms, put a check mark next to any term that meets the criterion. If some terms you want to teach are not found in the appendix, add them to your selection list.

Repeat this process for each of the other subject areas you will be teaching. If your selection list totals more than your original estimate, you will need to revise your plan. Let's say, for example, that after examining the terms in the appendix and adding other terms, you find that you have identified 45 mathematics terms, 20 science terms, 50 language arts terms, and 35 social studies terms—for a total of 150 terms. However, your goal was 120 terms. Now what?

One option is to increase the number of words you teach per week from four to five. Another option is to decrease the number of terms to be taught in one or more subject areas. For example, you could decrease the number of mathematics terms by 15 and the number of social studies terms by 15, bringing the total list down to your goal of 120 terms. Thus, instead of teaching 30 terms in each subject area, you would teach 30 mathematics terms, 20 science terms, 50 language arts terms, and 20 social studies terms. To generate this final list, you would have to identify the 30 most important mathematics terms out of your initial list of 45 and the 20 most important social studies terms out of your initial list of 35.

### Teaching a Single Subject to a Number of Classes

Middle schools, junior high schools, and high schools are usually organized by departments, so that a teacher is responsible for teaching a single subject, such as mathematics, to a number of classes. If you are a teacher in such an environment and you want to focus on terms from the national standards, use the same basic process as described in the previous paragraphs but consider terms for your subject area only.

To illustrate, let's say you are teaching a yearlong 8th grade mathematics course. To construct your list of academic vocabulary terms, begin by deciding how many terms you wish to teach in a given semester or year—for example, 3 terms per week for 30 weeks, for a total of 90 terms. Next, consult the Level 3 mathematics terms in Appendix B, answering the following question for each term: Is this term critically important to the mathematics content I will be teaching this year? Then, add terms that you consider important but did not find in the appendix. If your total number of selected terms exceeds your goal (in this case, 90 terms), revise your plan through one of two options: either delete some terms or increase your target number of terms.

## When Schools or Districts Choose the Terms

If the task of selecting and then systematically teaching academic terms is a **schoolwide** effort, the vocabulary program that emerges is more powerful than one created by an individual teacher for one class or subject area. If the approach is adopted **districtwide**, the program is even more powerful, for reasons such as the following:

- Students who change schools but stay within the same district can continue the program without interruption or variation in lists of terms.

- Effective teaching practices and other resources can be shared from school to school.

- District curriculum leaders, who possess a high level of knowledge in academic areas, as well as familiarity with local standards and curriculum materials, can be involved.

Because of these benefits, the discussion that follows generally applies to the context of a districtwide effort. If a districtwide approach is not feasible in your circumstances, however, the discussion translates easily to the context of a schoolwide effort.

## Organizing a Committee to Select the Academic Terms

If lists of terms are being created for an entire district, the committee that will create them should include both teachers and curriculum specialists from each subject area. If the lists are being created for a single school, teachers representing all grade levels should be on the committee. From the beginning, committee members should understand that the lists they make are not "cast in stone," but rather that additions and deletions may become necessary over time.

We recommend that the committee use the following process to generate the districtwide (or schoolwide) list of academic terms to be taught:

> *Phase 1:* Make decisions about the target number of words to be taught at each grade level and, by extension, across a grade-level interval (K–2, 3–5, 6–8, or 9–12) or a multigrade span (e.g., K–6 or K–12).

> *Phase 2:* For each academic content area in the program, create a rank-ordered list of words considered important to the grade-level interval or multigrade span by selecting words from Appendix B and adding words that reflect local standards and curriculum materials.

> *Phase 3:* Based on the length of these lists, determine how many terms should be taught in each academic area.

> *Phase 4:* Generate the final list of terms for each academic area by making additions, deletions, or other alterations.

> *Phase 5:* Assign terms to specific grades.

Let's consider each phase in some detail.

*Phase 1:* **Make decisions about the target number of words to be taught at each grade level and, by extension, across a grade-level interval (K–2, 3–5, 6–8, or 9–12) or a multigrade span (e.g., K–6 or K–12).**

During this phase, the committee addresses the issue of how many new terms should be introduced per week. To illustrate, let's say the committee is working on the terms for grades 3–5 and has determined that teachers at each grade level will introduce five new words per week, for 30 of the 36 weeks in the school year. Such a decision means that teachers would teach one word weekly in each of five content areas—mathematics, science, social studies, language arts, and health.

Extending this example, if words were distributed equally across all subject areas, 3rd grade teachers would teach 30 mathematics terms, 30 science terms, 30 social studies terms, 30 language arts terms, and 30 health terms over the course of the school year. The same number of words would be taught at grades 4 and 5. Therefore, the committee must identify 150 words at each grade level, or a total of 450 words for grades 3–5.

*Phase 2:* **For each academic content area in the program, create a rank-ordered list of words considered important to the grade-level interval or multigrade span by selecting words from the appendix and adding words that reflect local standards and curriculum materials.**

In this phase, the committee begins to select terms for specified grade levels and specified subject areas. Although this work can be completed in many ways, we recommend that committee members, individually, complete two tasks.

First, committee members should scan the appropriate terms in the appendix and rate each on a scale of 1–4 to reflect their individual opinions about including it on the district list, as follows:

**1** = The word should ***definitely not be*** on the district (or school) list.

**2** = The word should ***probably not be*** on the district (or school) list.

**3** = The word should ***probably be*** on the district (or school) list.

**4** = The word should ***definitely be*** on the district (or school) list.

Although this task takes some time, committee members will soon discover that they can rate many of the terms very quickly, especially those that are rated a 4 or a 1.

Second, committee members—again, as individuals—should generate a list of terms that they strongly feel should be on the district (or school) list but that do not appear in the appendix. The list in the appendix, although comprehensive, might not include terms that appear in a specific state's standards documents. Additionally, subject-matter specialists might believe that some terms should be taught even if they do not appear in their state standards documents.

When committee members have completed their individual ratings, the scores should be combined, beginning with the terms from the appendix. One option for combining the ratings is for the committee leader to call out each word; record each committee member's oral designation of the word as a 4, 3, 2, or 1; and tally the results. Another option is for the members to give their scores to someone who records, tallies, and aggregates the results for the committee. With either approach, each term will have a total score or average score based on the members' ratings.

Next, the committee should consider the additional words that committee members believe should be taught but that do not appear in the appendix. These recommended words should be combined into a new list and rated by each member according to the same four-point scale, with scores tallied as described previously.

The rating and tallying process will ultimately result in a rank-ordered list of terms that have been selected from Appendix B and generated by the committee. At this point, the committee may decide to include in the district list only those terms that have earned a designated minimum score, for example, an average rating of 3.5. This step would ensure that words appear on the final list only because they are considered important, not because they are needed to meet some arbitrarily decided upon number of terms for each subject area at each grade level. With this procedure, it is highly likely that the number of acceptable terms will be much greater for some academic content areas than for others; for example, in a particular grade-level interval, 200 social studies terms might meet the criterion but only 100 science terms.

***Phase 3:*** **Based on the length of these lists, determine how many terms should be taught in each academic area.**

To illustrate this phase, let's return to our example of the committee's work with grades 3–5. Let's assume that lists of terms have been generated for five content areas—mathematics, science, language arts, social studies, and health—and that when committee members examined the rank-ordered lists of words that met their criterion of a minimum score of 3.5, they found that the lists were considerably longer for some subject areas than for others. Let's also assume that in order to decide how the total number of words should be distributed among the content areas, they considered the relative length of the lists for each subject area. Their final decision might be, for example, that the words on the district list for the five subject areas should be distributed as follows: 30 percent from mathematics, 30 percent from social studies, 20 percent from science, and 10 percent each from language arts and health. Therefore, to implement the program for grades 3–5, which targeted a total of 450 terms across the entire interval, the committee would select approximately 135 words from mathematics, 135 from social studies, 90 from science, and 45 each from language arts and health.

We offer two cautionary notes here. First, when this work is done at the secondary level, with the grades 6–8 and 9–12 lists in Appendix B, it is likely that separate committees will work on each academic content area. Although this approach is certainly logical, it is possible that a committee representing a specific subject area might make decisions based on consideration of that subject only, rather than considering the total number of words that students are expected to learn across all content areas throughout the year. To avoid this scenario, districts should make sure that subject-specific committees communicate with one another and make decisions in the context of an academic vocabulary program that targets all subject areas.

Second, a committee should treat all calculations in this phase of the process as approximations only. For instance, in our illustration of the committee working with grades 3–5, if the committee members felt strongly that some critical words were being excluded to avoid making the district list too long, they might reconsider their initial decision that five words be taught per week for 30 weeks. Instead, they might adopt the convention that *six* words will be taught each week, across all classes, for a period of 30 weeks. This modest increase would mean that an additional 90 terms could be included on the final district list across three grade levels (i.e., 1 word x 30 weeks x 3 grade levels).

### Phase 4: Generate the final list of terms for each academic area by making additions, deletions, or other alterations.

In this phase, the committee uses its approximate calculations and the rank-ordered lists generated in the preceding phases to create the final district list. If the committee members in our example have determined that 135 words will be taught in mathematics across grades 3, 4, and 5, then they will include the first 135 words from the rank-ordered list in the final districtwide list.

### Phase 5: Assign terms to specific grades.

As mentioned previously, we have organized the 7,923 terms in Appendix B of this manual into four grade-level intervals: K–2, 3–5, 6–8, and 9–12. We use these intervals because the specific grade level at which a specific term should be taught is not absolute. For example, a term that might best be taught at the 5th grade level in one school district might be more appropriately taught at the 6th grade level in another district. Therefore, the appendix provides a *band* of grade levels that are appropriate for each term. Within those grade-level bands, the committee must identify at which grades specific terms should be taught. Although this task requires work, it allows the committee to customize an academic vocabulary program to meet the district's specific needs.

The committee can complete this final task by having each member work individually and then pool the results, however, we recommend that the committee work as a group. Returning one last time to our committee working with grades 3–5, let's assume that the members have identified 90 science words as a result of the first four phases of the selection process. Committee members would now reexamine each term, decide which terms are basic to the understanding of other terms on the list, and assign these to be taught at the earlier grade levels. The committee could begin by identifying the 30 words on the list that are the most basic, and place these 30 terms on the 3rd grade list. Then, they would identify the 30 terms that are the next most basic, and these would be taught at the 4th grade level. The remaining 30 words would become the list for 5th grade students to learn.

# Getting Started

The goal of the five-phase process we have just described is to create an agreed-upon list of terms to be taught at specific grade levels. We recognize, however, that many factors can delay the forming of a committee and scheduling of the work time needed to compile such a list. The good news is that having a completed list is not necessary in order to begin! **Individual teachers or small teams who wish to implement the program early can start using the instructional processes recommended in this manual right away.** We recommend that they select a few terms from the appendix that they feel confident will be on the final list and begin teaching these terms in their classrooms as a "pilot" program. In so doing, they will learn a great deal about the day-to-day workings of a comprehensive approach to academic vocabulary development; their experiences will provide guidance to the committee charged with constructing the final district list; and their students will benefit in significant and lasting ways.

# 3 | Teaching the Selected Terms

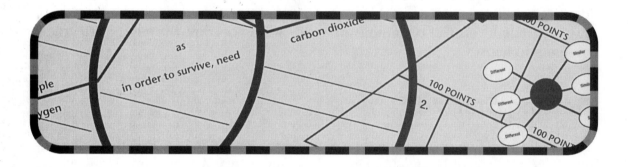

With the background work of selecting the terms completed, the focus turns to teaching those terms. Although the background work must be done in order to design and implement a comprehensive academic vocabulary program, the ultimate success or failure of the program will depend on the quality of instruction teachers provide. This chapter provides specific recommendations for teaching the selected terms.

## A Six-Step Process for Teaching New Terms

The six-step process described below will guide the direct instruction for the targeted academic terms. The first three steps, used as a set, ensure that teachers appropriately introduce a new term and help students develop an initial understanding of it. The last three steps describe different types of multiple exposures that students should experience over time to help them shape and sharpen their understanding of the terms.

> *Step 1:* Provide a description, explanation, or example of the new term.

> *Step 2:* Ask students to restate the description, explanation, or example in their own words.

*Step 3:* Ask students to construct a picture, symbol, or graphic representing the term.

*Step 4:* Engage students periodically in activities that help them add to their knowledge of the terms in their notebooks.

*Step 5:* Periodically ask students to discuss the terms with one another.

*Step 6:* Involve students periodically in games that allow them to play with terms.

## *Step 1:* Provide a description, explanation, or example of the new term.

This first step simply states that students need some initial information about the term that they are learning. Before providing this information, however, try to determine what students already know about it. You might simply ask students to share aloud what they already know or what they *think* they know. If students do have some knowledge of the term, carefully listen to their responses because you can use what they say in your initial presentation. For example, you might hear misconceptions that you will need to clarify. You might also hear *accurate* prior knowledge of the term that you can build on as you present the new information.

Once you have determined what students already know about the term, help them build an initial understanding of the term. Although this first step states that you should "provide" information to the students, this does not necessarily mean that you will stand at the front of the class and deliver that information. You can help students build their initial understanding of the term in a number of different ways, including

- Introduce direct experiences, such as a field trip or a guest speaker, that provide examples of the term.
- Tell a story that integrates the term.
- Use video or computer images as the stimulus for understanding the information.
- Ask individual students, or small groups, to do some initial investigation into the term and present the information—perhaps in the form of a skit or pantomime—to the class.
- Use current events to help make the term applicable to something familiar to students.
- Describe your own mental pictures of the term.
- Find or create pictures that exemplify the term.

Notice that some of these suggestions include providing images. Using both linguistic and nonlinguistic approaches will help students not only begin to develop an initial understanding of the term, but will also help prepare them to create their own pictures, a requirement of Step 3.

It is important to emphasize that this first step does not involve presenting students with a *definition* of a term or asking them to look up the definition in the dictionary. We describe in depth the logic behind this strategy in *Building Background Knowledge for Academic Achievement*. Briefly, the reason is that a description, explanation, or example provides students with a more natural starting place for learning a new term. Generally speaking, when people first learn a word, they don't have a formal understanding of it, such as they would find in a dictionary, but only a general understanding that is quite informal. It makes sense, therefore, to introduce the meaning of a term in an informal way, much as one friend would describe it to another friend.

To illustrate, let's assume that a mathematics teacher is introducing the term *function*. During this first step, the teacher might provide a brief description such as the following:

> A function is a relationship between two things like height and weight. As one goes up, the other goes up. Isn't it generally true that as you have grown in height over the years, your weight has also gone up? We could describe this relationship by saying, "Your weight is a function of your height."

Although the teacher's explanation does not provide students with a complete accounting of the characteristics of a function, it does provide a viable starting place for learning the term. In later stages of the six-step process, you will ask students to go back to terms that have been introduced and add to their initial understanding, correcting any misconceptions from that initial understanding.

You will notice that some of the terms in Appendix B are proper nouns—for example, *The Iliad* and *The Odyssey*. If proper nouns are on your district's list, provide students with an initial explanation that includes only the information considered important to those specific proper nouns. For instance, including *The Iliad* and *The Odyssey* on a district's list implies that all students in the district are expected to have a general understanding of these epic poems, not necessarily to read them. You could assume that the poems were placed on the list because they are considered important background knowledge for academic success in a specific subject area—in this case, history.

When you present proper nouns to students as academic vocabulary terms, you would first identify the characteristics necessary for students to develop a general understanding of the term. In the example of *The Iliad* and *The Odyssey*, you might decide that students should know that the purpose of the poems was to provide Greeks of the 7th and 8th centuries B.C. with information about the adventures of Odysseus and, probably more important, about the gods and goddesses important in their society. In addition, you might want students to know that the poems are associated with Homer, although many scholars believe that they were probably written by several people and that Homer might not have been a real person.

The book *Building Background Knowledge for Academic Achievement* provides specific guidance on how to determine the important characteristics for terms that you teach. The point here is that with the important characteristics identified for a selected proper noun, you would be able to present the information in an easily understood form. In the case of *The Iliad* and *The Odyssey*, you might relate the information as a simple description of their place in Greek life:

> In Greece during the 7th and 8th centuries B.C., two poems were immensely popular and were taught to all Greek citizens. They were *The Iliad* and *The Odyssey*.

------

### Additional examples for Step 1

- Mr. Collier noticed that the science book glossary defined climate as follows: "The prevailing meteorological conditions, or weather, of a place, including temperature, precipitation, and wind." Instead of using that definition, he explained the term this way: "Climate is the word that describes what weather is generally like in a particular place. If someone says that a place has a warm, dry climate, it means that the winters are not really cold and there is probably not much snow, plus the summers are probably pretty hot without much rain."

- Janie listened as her teacher explained who Louis Pasteur was: "Look at your milk container and you will see the word *pasteurized*. That word means that the milk was heated to kill the bacteria that could make you sick. Louis Pasteur, a man from France, invented the process to make milk safe to drink in the 1800s. That process was then named after him."

------

### *Step 2:* Ask students to restate the description, explanation, or example in their own words.

When you ask students to restate in their own words what has been presented in the introduction to the term, it is critical that they do not simply copy what you have said, but that they construct their own descriptions, explanations, or examples. Their constructions need not be comprehensive, but efforts should be made to ensure a lack of major errors. Monitor students' work and help them clear up any confusions or major errors as they work. Remember, however, that throughout the process of learning new terms, students will have a number of opportunities to shape and sharpen their understanding. In other words, their initial understanding can be, and probably will be, quite rudimentary.

If students struggle with restating the description, explanation, or examples in their own words, you might consider doing some of the following:

- Go back and provide additional descriptions, explanations, or examples.

- Allow students to discuss the term with a partner or in a small group.

- If they have the general idea but are struggling with stating what they are thinking, you might move on to Step 3 and ask them to create a nonlinguistic representation and then go back to the linguistic description.

Ask students to record their descriptions, explanations, and examples in their academic notebooks. The student notebooks accommodate more than one vocabulary term per page, which can be labeled for different content areas. Figure 3.1 depicts the format for the notebook pages. We discuss the role of the academic notebook in depth in Chapter 5.

Students write their own descriptions, explanations, or examples of the new term in the space provided. Figure 3.2 contains an example of a student's explanation of the term *function*.

Notice that in Figure 3.2, and in the additional examples in the box below, the students' descriptions are not comprehensive or even completely accurate, but they all represent a starting place for the students' gradual shaping and sharpening of their understanding of the term *function*.

---

### Additional Examples of Step 2

- Jackson explained *percent* in his academic notebook this way:

  Percent means how many things there are out of 100 things. 75 percent means 75 out of 100.

- Sophie's entry for *Native American* included the following:

  Native means the first people who lived somewhere, so Native American means the first people who lived in America. They lived here before it was called America. We used to call them Indians, but that did not make sense. They weren't from India.

---

Term: _____ | My Understanding: | 1 | 2 | 3 | 4 | Subject:

Describe: _____

_____

_____

_____

Draw:

Term: _____ | My Understanding: | 1 | 2 | 3 | 4 |

Describe: _____

_____

_____

_____

Draw:

**Figure 3.1 | Sample Notebook Page**

Term: **Function**                    | My Understanding:    | 1 | 2 | 3 | 4

Describe: It's when one thing makes another happen or one thing goes up the same way that another goes up.

Draw:

Subject:

Term: _____                 | My Understanding:    | 1 | 2 | 3 | 4

Describe:

Draw:

Figure 3.2 | **Student Description of** *Function*

By design, if the program is used districtwide, the students' academic notebooks will eventually contain all of the important terms taught in every subject area at every grade level. Thus, teachers and students can refer to terms in different subject areas. For example, a middle school student who has classes in mathematics, science, social studies, and language arts would have a section in his academic notebook for each of these subjects. The mathematics teacher can have students refer to some of the science terms that were taught, the social studies teacher can refer to some of the mathematics terms, and so on.

### *Step 3:* Ask students to construct a picture, symbol, or graphic representing the term or phrase.

When you ask students to construct a picture, symbol, or graphic representation of a term, they are forced to think of the term in a totally different way. Written or oral descriptions require students to process information in linguistic ways. Pictures, symbols, and graphic representations require students to process information in nonlinguistic ways. Consult *Building Background Knowledge for Academic Achievement* for a thorough discussion of the reasons why constructing graphics is such an effective learning activity.

As Figure 3.1 shows, the pages of the academic notebook include a place for students to draw their nonlinguistic representations for each term. As an example, Figure 3.3 shows one student's nonlinguistic depiction of the term *function.*

If students are not accustomed to creating pictures and graphics for ideas, they might, initially, need significant guidance and modeling. Even if they have experience with nonlinguistic representations, it is likely that they will still need help with terms that are new to them, difficult, or abstract.

Following are some examples of the types of challenges you might face during Step 3, and suggestions for overcoming them:

**Challenge: Students believe they cannot draw.**

*Suggestions:*

- Model, model, model.
- Provide examples of students' drawings and your own drawings that are rough but that represent the ideas.
- Allow students, at first, to work together.

**Challenge: Students try to "overdraw."**

*Suggestions:*

- Model, model, model.

Term: **Function**                    | My Understanding: | 1 | 2 | ③ | 4 | Subject:

Describe: It's when one thing makes another happen or one thing goes up the same way that another goes up.

Draw:

Term: _____                    | My Understanding: | 1 | 2 | 3 | 4 |

Describe: _____

Draw:

Figure 3.3 | **Student Graphic Representation of *Function***

- Play "Draw Me" (see Chapter 4) and allow students to share tips on "quick draws" needed to play the game.

- Present a lesson on the difference between drawing and sketching.

**Challenge: Students would rather just copy the written definition.**

*Suggestions:*

- Discuss with them the power of pictures.

- Allow students to work together.

- Ask students to share personal stories of how pictures have helped them learn.

**Challenge: The students—and you—are having trouble depicting the term.**

*Suggestions:*

- You might have to practice and help students practice, because different types of terms require different types of pictures.

- Go to the Internet and search for images for the term.

This last challenge is a reminder that as you and your students focus on different terms, it will become clear that some terms are more difficult to depict than others. Through practice, you and your students will discover the many ways to illustrate meaning with pictures. The following are some useful approaches to creating nonlinguistic representations:

- Sometimes you can **draw the actual thing** that is represented by the term. Figure 3.4, for example, depicts *diameter*.

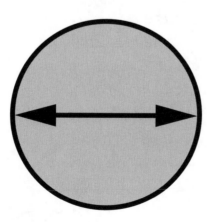

Figure 3.4 | *Diameter*

- Sometimes students can **draw a symbol** for the word. Figure 3.5 and Figure 3.6 are commonly accepted symbols for DNA and justice respectively.

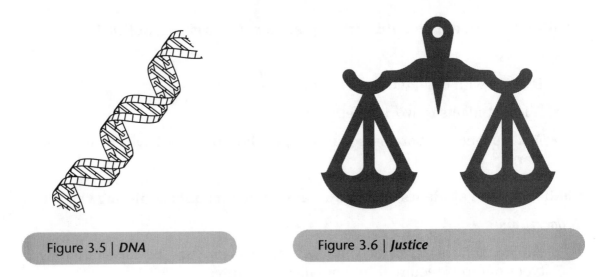

Figure 3.5 | *DNA*

Figure 3.6 | *Justice*

- You might encourage students to **draw an example** of the term. Consider Figure 3.7, which shows a student's illustration for the term *food chain*.

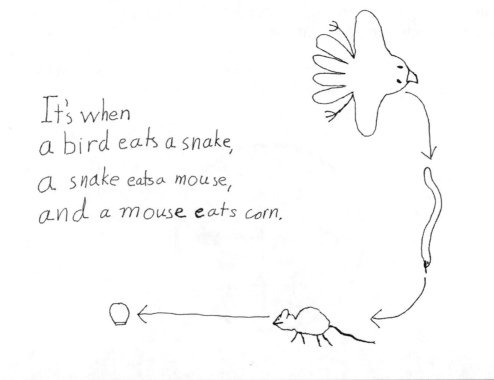

It's when a bird eats a snake, a snake eats a mouse, and a mouse eats corn.

Figure 3.7 | *Food Chain*

- Some words can be **represented with graphics**. For example, students might understand the general meaning of *decentralization*, but they might not have any idea how to draw it. If they are familiar with how to use shapes and arrows, they could depict the meaning of the term (and its root word, *centralization*), as shown in Figure 3.8.

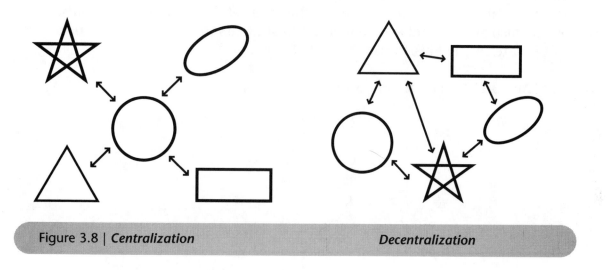

Figure 3.8 | *Centralization*                    *Decentralization*

- Students can often **dramatize the term** by using cartoon bubbles that help to reveal its meanings. For the music term *synthesize*, a student might draw Figure 3.9.

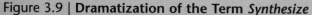

Figure 3.9 | **Dramatization of the Term** *Synthesize*

Keep in mind also that it is not necessary for students to draw everything free-hand. Figure 3.10 shows how a student could trace a map of India to indicate the approximate location of New Delhi.

Although it is recommended that students develop the ability to create pictures and graphics for the terms, you might sometimes need to allow them to use pictures they find in print materials or on the Internet. Further, to ensure success, you can also allow—and even encourage—students to work with their peers to represent terms that are particularly challenging.

See Figure 3.11 for additional examples of Step 3.

New Delhi, India

Figure 3.10 | **Hand-Traced Map of India**

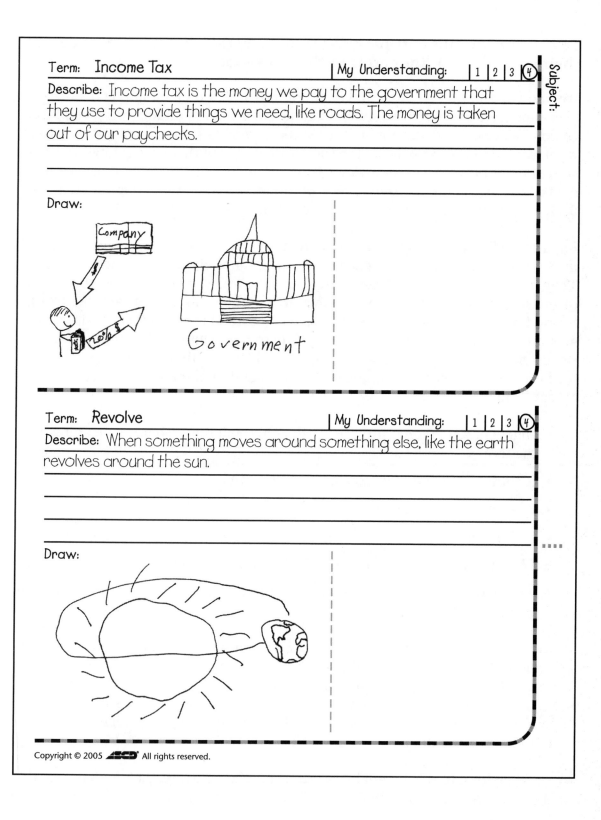

Term: Income Tax | My Understanding: 1 2 3 ④ Subject:

Describe: Income tax is the money we pay to the government that they use to provide things we need, like roads. The money is taken out of our paychecks.

Draw:

Company

Government

Term: Revolve | My Understanding: 1 2 3 ④

Describe: When something moves around something else, like the earth revolves around the sun.

Draw:

Figure 3.11 | **Additional Examples of Step 3**

## *Step 4:* Engage students periodically in activities that help them add to their knowledge of the terms in their notebooks

We know from both research and common sense that understanding deepens over time if students continually reexamine their understanding of a given term. Of course, when students encounter the terms during subject area courses, they will have the opportunity to add to their knowledge of the terms. However, this step of the process suggests that activities should be planned that engage students explicitly in the focused review of targeted terms. A number of activities designed to provide these opportunities are described in Chapter 4.

Each time students engage in these activities, they should be provided opportunities to add to, or revise, the entry for the term in their academic notebooks. They might make these changes in two places. First, they might want to add to, or revise, their initial description of the term or their initial picture of the word. Second, students might use the extra space provided in the bottom right-hand section of each term's entry (see Figure 3.1) to highlight new information and record new insights. That space has been left blank so that students can use it for different purposes, depending on the term and on their learning needs. For example, they might

- Highlight a prefix or suffix that will help them remember the meaning of the term.

- Identify synonyms or antonyms for the term.

- Draw an additional picture or graphic.

- List related words.

- Write brief cautions or reminders of common confusions.

- Translate the term into another language, if English is the student's second language.

If students were reviewing the term *capital* in the social studies section of their notebooks, for instance, they might decide to write in the extra space, "Remember capitol, with an O, always refers to the building." If they were reviewing the science term *symbiosis*, they might add, "Related words: mutualism and parasitism." If they were reexamining the math term *addition*, they might write, "Antonym—subtraction."

Again, Chapter 4 of this manual describes specific activities that you can use to guide students to enhance their understanding of the terms in their notebooks.

### *Step 5:* Periodically ask students to discuss the terms with one another.

Research and common sense also lead us to Step 5 because they confirm that interacting with other people about what we are learning deepens the understanding of everyone involved—particularly when we are learning new terms. Therefore, you should periodically give students opportunities to engage in such interactions.

Although their discussions can be informal and unstructured, you might sometimes want to provide a structure. One such structure, modeled after the **Think-Pair-Share strategy** often used in teacher workshops, can be an effective guide.

**Think:** Provide a few minutes of quiet "think time" to allow students, individually, to review their own descriptions and images of the targeted terms in their notebooks. Consider modeling for them by "thinking aloud" some things they might consider during this quiet time.

**Pair:** After students have had a chance to think about the targeted terms, organize them into pairs and ask them to discuss their descriptions and pictures of the terms with their partners. You might need to guide these interactions by suggesting or modeling ways they can discuss the terms, which may include

- Comparing their descriptions of the term.

- Describing their pictures to each other.

- Explaining to each other any new information they have learned or any "Aha's!" they have experienced since the last time they reviewed the terms.

- Identifying areas of disagreement or confusion and seeking clarification.

Ask students not to change their entries in their notebooks yet. At this point in the process, they should simply be discussing their understanding of the terms.

**Share:** Invite students to share aloud with the whole class any new thoughts or understandings they have discussed in their pairs. As students share, highlight interesting ideas and encourage students to explain any examples of confusions or misconceptions that surfaced during their discussions. This step provides an opportunity for you to make sure that confusions and misconceptions have been resolved accurately.

After the Think-Pair-Share experience, ask students to make additions and revisions to their notebook entries. Monitor their work to ensure that their additions and revisions are accurate.

Notice that one of the major goals of Step 5 is to encourage students to help each other identify and clear up misconceptions and confusion. This goal communicates to students that it is normal for their initial understanding of an idea to be incomplete or flawed. They should see that discussing the terms with their peers helps them to detect their errors and correct their work.

The activities in this step need not follow the strategy we have just described. They can be unstructured and student-directed, if you wish, or structured with a different method.

### Step 6: Involve students periodically in games that allow them to play with terms.

Games are one of the most underused instructional tools in education. Many types of games can help you keep new terms in the forefront of students' thinking and allow students to reexamine their understanding of terms. Set aside blocks of time each week to play games, or use them spontaneously throughout the day to energize students and guide them in the review and use of important terms. For example, a variation of the popular game *Pictionary* is a format that engages students and helps them to review and recreate images for targeted terms. Specific games are described in detail in Chapter 4 of this manual.

## Scheduling Time for Academic Vocabulary Instruction

Although many teachers include some vocabulary instruction in their instructional plans, the six-step process described above requires a much more regular, systematic approach to planning. Teachers must block out time for the direct instruction described in the first three steps of the process, and decide how often and when the activities in the last three steps will be used. (We consider scheduling time for Steps 4, 5, and 6 in Chapter 5 of this manual.) These planning decisions will vary from teacher to teacher and will differ somewhat in elementary versus secondary settings. This fact notwithstanding, we offer some general suggestions for scheduling time for academic vocabulary instruction.

First, you might decide when and how often you will present new terms. You might, for example, determine that you can present three new terms in about 15 minutes. That is, it takes you about 15 minutes to guide the students through the first three steps of the process for three terms. Although this might seem like a fairly short period of time, remember that the initial steps only require that students begin to gain a familiarity with the term.

Let's say you decide that you want to begin by introducing three new terms a week for three weeks, and then add three new terms every other week after that. During a nine-week period, students would be presented with 18 words to enter in their notebooks. After this strong beginning, you might decide to introduce fewer terms in the next nine weeks, so that you can focus more on Steps 4, 5, and 6, which help students review terms. This pattern would then be repeated or revised, depending on the needs of your students.

## Monitoring the Accuracy of Student Work

It should be clear by now that, with guidance and modeling, students are generating their own descriptions and nonlinguistic representations for the terms they are learning. They record their initial understandings of the terms and then periodically add to or revise their descriptions and nonlinguistic representations.

Although the six-step teaching process specifically recommends that misconceptions be identified and clarified (see Step 5), it is important to monitor the accuracy and clarity of students' work throughout the process. You can do so in a variety of ways:

- **Whenever students are working with their notebooks, move around the room and look at their work.** In this way, you can catch individual students' errors and correct them quickly. You can also discover patterns of misconceptions and call the class back together for additional instruction, if necessary. You might need to ask some students to cross out their initial work and create a completely new, accurate entry for a term. If they complain about this, explain again that, because these terms have been identified as critical to their success in school and in life, accuracy and clarity are essential.

- **Periodically check students' notebooks to determine the level of accuracy and clarity in their work.** You might make a commitment to check a few notebooks per week, with the goal of reviewing every notebook regularly. Or, especially if you are a secondary teacher, you might randomly select notebooks to review. This review will give you an overall impression of how well students are learning targeted terms. Periodic quizzes, described in the next section, could then be used to monitor all students.

- **During the review activities and games (see Steps 4, 5, and 6 above), listen for misconceptions and areas of confusion.** You might try to correct or clarify errors at the time you hear them, or you might want to make note of what you observe and then address the issue during your next scheduled vocabulary instruction time.

- **Encourage students to collaborate as a class to ensure that everyone is learning the terms accurately.** Often, students' peers can identify and clear up misconceptions better than a teacher can.

## Keeping Track of Students' Progress

Students like to observe their progress over time as they learn new terms. One simple and nonthreatening way to help students track their progress is to encourage them to self-assess. We recommend that you provide students with a set of criteria like that depicted in Figure 3.12.

As you can see, the scale in Figure 3.12 portrays levels of understanding that range from having knowledge beyond what was presented in class to feeling so uncertain about the term that the student has little or no understanding of it.

To help students determine their level of knowledge regarding specific terms, you can give periodic quizzes. Instead of simply scoring students' responses as correct or incorrect and recording their scores in a grade book, however, you can review the answers in class and allow students to score their own responses according to the scale depicted in Figure 3.12. After each quiz, students would indicate their level of understanding of each word tested by circling 1, 2, 3, or 4 at the right-hand side of the word entry in their notebooks.

To help students determine how well they are learning the vocabulary terms in general, you can periodically ask them to create a visual representation of their progress by creating a chart such as the one shown in Figure 3.13. Filling out this chart would require the students to go through the pages of their notebooks and count the number of terms for which they have rated their own level of

| Knowledge Level | Description |
|---|---|
| **Level 4** | I understand even more about the term than I was taught. |
| **Level 3** | I understand the term and I'm not confused about any part of what it means. |
| **Level 2** | I'm a little uncertain about what the term means, but I have a general idea. |
| **Level 1** | I'm very uncertain about the term. I really don't understand what it means. |

Figure 3.12 | **Scale for Self-Evaluation of Knowledge of Terms**

| Student Progress Chart | | | | |
|---|---|---|---|---|
| Date: November 4 | | | | |
| # of Items | Level 4 | Level 3 | Level 2 | Level 1 |
| 30 | | | | |
| . | | | | |
| . | | | | |
| 14 | | | | |
| 13 | | | | |
| 12 | | | | |
| 11 | | | X | |
| 10 | | X | X | |
| 9 | | X | X | |
| 8 | | X | X | |
| 7 | | X | X | X |
| 6 | | X | X | X |
| 5 | X | X | X | X |
| 4 | X | X | X | X |
| 3 | X | X | X | X |
| 2 | X | X | X | X |
| 1 | X | X | X | X |

Figure 3.13 | **Student Progress Chart**

understanding as 4, then the number of terms that are rated as 3, and so on. The chart creates a little histogram of their learning. In the example in Figure 3.13, the chart shows that the student understands five terms at level 4, ten terms at level 3, eleven terms at level 2, and seven words at level 1. Once a month (or so), the student might complete a new chart. Over time, the total number of terms will increase, but students can still compare their charts to see how they are progressing.

Of course, you can also give periodic tests on terms as part of students' grades in the subject area. Be careful when designing these tests, however, because the six-step teaching process we have described allows for great variation in the ways students describe and represent terms. Consequently, a multiple-choice or matching test might not be a valid assessment, especially if words within the test items are unfamiliar to the student. We recommend constructing tests with open-ended questions that allow the students to show what they understand about the terms. To score the test items, you can adapt the self-assessment rubric shown in Figure 3.12.

Also, if you use a rubric to score items on a test, avoid translating the scores into a percentage for the final test grade. Let's say a test has 30 items; with a four-point rubric, the total possible points would equal 120. Now, consider a student who scores a 3 on every term tested, meaning that she has a solid understanding of all of the terms. In the traditional percentage scale (90–100 percent=*A*, 80–89 percent=*B*, and so on), the student's total score of 90 would be 75 percent of the total possible points and, thus, she would receive a *C* on the test—perhaps not an accurate reflection of her level of knowledge. Furthermore, students who might earn a 2 for each item, meaning they have "a little confusion" but have a general understanding of each term, would, if traditional percentages were calculated, receive an *F*. Therefore, if you use a rubric for scoring test items, you should use an average rubric score—not a percentage—for the final grade on the test.

## Working with ESL Students

The six steps described in this chapter are written from the perspective of teaching new terms to students who are native English speakers. However, they can be modified to work well with students who are learning English as a second language (ESL). Such students are also referred to as English language learners (ELL students), but we will use the abbreviation ESL in the following discussion.

Before considering each of the six steps from this perspective, however, we should consider a question that frequently is asked regarding such students. That question deals with the perceived need for these students to focus on high-frequency, functional words they will encounter in general reading, for example: *dinner, lavatory,* and *bus schedule.* The issue of teaching high-frequency words such as these is addressed in depth in the book *Building Background Knowledge for Academic Achievement.* We encourage you to read the discussion contained therein. Although directly teaching these words to ESL students certainly has some merit, we believe that its utility is somewhat overstated for at least two reasons. First, these words are encountered frequently enough in the written language that they will most likely be learned if students read fiction or nonfiction materials that are of interest to them. In fact, although this manual focuses only on direct instruction in academic terms, having students read fiction and nonfiction for the purpose of learning high-frequency terms is an integral part of the approach described in *Building Background Knowledge for Academic Achievement.* Consequently, we recommend that a systematic program of wide reading be implemented along with the program of direct instruction in academic terms described in this manual. If executed well, a program of wide reading can help ESL students learn high-frequency terms that are important to general literacy development.

The second reason teaching high-frequency words is not emphasized in this manual is that vocabulary programs that emphasize high-frequency terms for ESL students commonly fail to address the important academic terms that students encounter in their content area courses. In effect, thanks to a well intended but misguided attempt to allow them to learn the "easier" terms first, ESL students never receive systematic instruction in the more difficult academic terms. The approach described here assumes that ESL students are well equipped to learn academic terms at the highest level of complexity. However, the instructional sequence must be adapted to allow ESL students to use the background knowledge encoded in their native language. The six steps described below provide for this allowance.

### *Step 1 (ESL):* Provide a description, explanation, or example of the new term (along with a nonlinguistic representation).

This first step of the six-step instructional process differs dramatically for ESL students. Ideally, your description, explanation, or example should be given in the students' native language. This makes intuitive sense, because students start to learn any new term by making connections with things they already know. Obviously, it is difficult, if not impossible, for learners to make such connections when a new term is being taught in a language unfamiliar to them.

If you cannot provide the description, explanation, or example of a new term in your students' native language, the best alternative is to pair students of the same native language or organize students into triads. It is imperative that one member of each pair or triad be comfortable with English or at least have some facility with it. The English-speaking student can then help her partners who are not as proficient in English. If no student has proficiency in both languages, then the next option is to solicit assistance from a bilingual paraprofessional or parent who would work with the ESL students to help them understand the initial description, explanation, or example.

Also during this first step, it is useful to provide students with some form of non-linguistic representation of the term you are teaching. (Recall that in the previous discussion of the six-step process, a nonlinguistic representation was elicited in Step 3 when students were asked to create their own nonlinguistic representation.) Giving ESL students a nonlinguistic representation in Step 1 will provide a way for them to understand the meaning of the term that is not dependent on an understanding of English. For a concrete term such as *angle* or *sea wall*, your nonlinguistic representation might be just a simple sketch, but more abstract terms, such as *slavery*, will be harder to depict. Nevertheless, make every effort to provide some type of nonlinguistic representation. To represent *slavery*, for instance, you might provide some pictures downloaded from the Internet depicting slavery in the United States. Although ESL students might not benefit very much from verbal explanations, the nonlinguistic representation (i.e., the pictures) of slavery would provide at least some basis for understanding the term.

### *Step 2 (ESL):* Ask students to restate the description, explanation, or example in their own words.

Permit ESL students to write the description, explanation, or example in their native language, unless they feel comfortable using English or prefer to use English. Again, the reason for this is straightforward. Learning a term involves integrating the new information into an existing knowledge base. If a student's existing knowledge base is encoded in Spanish, then Spanish is the most appropriate vehicle for describing new information. Allowing students to use their native language also communicates a basic respect for their language and their culture. It is also appropriate to encourage ESL students to record any English terms they are familiar with that are related to the term being presented. Thus, ESL students would first encode new terms in their native language but also encode the term using familiar English words.

### *Step 3 (ESL):* Ask students to construct a picture, symbol, or graphic representing the term or phrase.

This step is particularly important for ESL students. Whereas they might be constrained in their ability to devise a linguistic description, explanation, or example, they will not be constrained in their ability to create a nonlinguistic representation such as a picture, pictograph, or graph. Recall that the teacher has also provided a nonlinguistic representation for students in Step 1. It is important that students be encouraged to create their own representations and not simply copy the one provided by the teacher. These representations will most likely reflect the students' native culture, which is exactly the intent. Learning academic terms involves making connections with things familiar to us, and these things commonly arise from experiences native to our culture.

### *Step 4 (ESL):* Engage students periodically in activities that help them add to their knowledge of the terms in their notebooks.

As much as possible, allow ESL students to engage in these activities in their native language. Let's assume that you present students with the following incomplete analogy:

Bar graph is to pie chart as _____ is to _____.

A native Spanish-speaking student, for example, should be allowed to complete the analogy in Spanish.

*Step 5 (ESL):* **Periodically ask students to discuss the terms with one another.**

This step is a perfect opportunity to pair students of the same native language or to place students together in triads. Ideally, at least one student in a pair or triad will have a working knowledge of English, and these bilingual students can help those who are more monolingual bridge the gap between their native language and English. If bilingual students are not available, then the next option is to use bilingual paraprofessionals or parents who are willing to help.

*Step 6 (ESL):* **Involve students periodically in games that allow them to play with terms.**

In this step, again, try to organize students of the same native language into pairs or triads. The bilingual members of these pairs or triads can facilitate the games for their more monolingual partners. If bilingual students are not available, solicit help from bilingual paraprofessionals or parents.

## Summary

This chapter has provided specific recommendations for teaching academic vocabulary, including a six-step process for teaching new terms to students. Key to this process is the use of the student notebooks. In their notebooks, students record new terms and an initial description of each term. Over time, they add new information as their understanding of the terms deepens and matures.

# 4 | Review Activities and Games

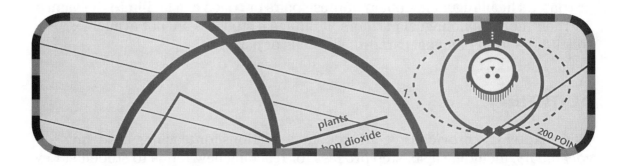

The six-step process for teaching academic terms introduced in Chapter 3 suggests that you engage students in activities and games that will help them add to their knowledge as they review and play with the terms they have recorded in their notebooks (see Steps 4 and 6). This chapter describes specific activities for Step 4 and specific games for Step 6

The format for each vocabulary term's entry in the student notebooks includes a space for students to self-assess using a rubric that describes levels of understanding. After engaging students in activities and games like those presented in this chapter, prompt them to go through their notebooks and decide whether they have increased their understanding of any of the terms.

## Activities for Step 4

Step 4 of the six-step process indicates that it is important to give students opportunities to reexamine their understanding of the academic terms that have been presented to them. You can use the review strategies provided in this chapter during a concentrated block of time set aside for review, as the focus of a homework assignment, or as quick five-minute refreshers interspersed throughout the day.

**Review Activity**

# Free Association

## Description

This is perhaps the quickest and most unstructured of the review activities. It involves asking students simply to say any words that they think of when they hear a particular term. For example, upon hearing *fraction*, students might respond with words such as *decimal*, *numerator*, *denominator*, *half*, *thirds*, *parts*, *whole*, *invert*, and so on.

## Procedure

During a designated vocabulary block, or spontaneously at any time during the day, announce that it is "free-association time." You then call out a term—the target—and ask students to take turns—as a class, in small groups, or in pairs—saying any word they think of that is related to the target term. After a few seconds, say, "Stop." The last person to say a word must explain how that word is related to the target.

---

**Target Term:** Requirements for life

**Related Words:**

| | |
|---|---|
| water | warmth |
| food | homes |
| shelter | family |
| oxygen | friends |
| air | society |

---

An alternative to oral free association is to ask students to write their responses in a learning log or on scratch paper. When you say, "Stop," they exchange papers with a partner and ask each other to explain any of the words on their lists. In this way, students generate their own lists, but also are exposed to the thinking of another student.

---

**Tip:** If you do this activity aloud with an entire class, things can become chaotic. Set some parameters. For example, require that students raise their hands and be called on, or, to ensure that they pay attention to their peers' responses, require that they repeat the previous student's response before offering their own.

## Review Activity

# Comparing Terms

### Description

A number of formats can be used to guide students through the process of comparing terms from their notebooks. We have included brief descriptions and examples of four different formats: sentence stems, the Venn diagram, double bubble, and the matrix.

**Sentence Stems**

This format provides sentences to be completed by students. The first set of sentences asks students to fill in similarities between the two terms, and the second set asks for differences.

Sentence stems provide very structured guidance for students, thus helping them to avoid common errors in their thinking. Sometimes, for example, students jump into a comparison task without first identifying the characteristics on which they will base their comparison.

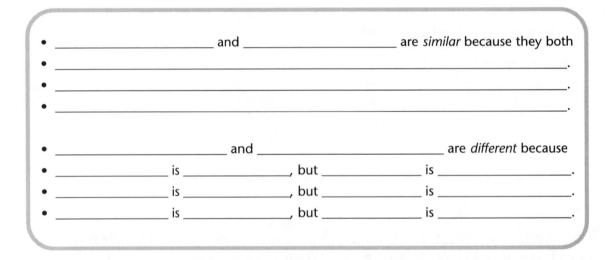

Comparisons begin to sound like this: "Items A and B are different because Item A is blue but Item B is round." These two differences do not focus on the same characteristic; one descriptor relates to color and the other relates to shape. The sentence stem format helps students to maintain focus on the same general characteristics simply because of the syntax of the sentence. See the examples below.

*Monarchy* and *dictatorship* are similar because they both
- Are forms of government.
- Are governments with major power given to one person.
- Have examples from history in which the powerful person was a tyrant.

*Monarchy* and *dictatorship* are different because
- In a *monarchy*, the ruler is often in power because of heritage, but in a *dictatorship*, the ruler often comes to power through force or coercion.
- In *monarchies* today, the rulers are often perceived to be loved by the people, but in *dictatorships*, the rulers are often feared and hated by the people.
- A *monarchy* can coexist with a representative government, but a *dictatorship* often is a police state.

*The sun* and *the moon* are similar because they both
- Are in space.
- Influence our lives and our moods.
- Shine.

*The sun* and *the moon* are different because
- The sun is about 93 million miles away from Earth, but the moon is only about 250,000 miles away.
- The sun is made of gases, but the moon is made of rocks.
- The sun influences the temperature, but the moon influences ocean waves.

**Venn Diagram**

The Venn diagram is another format commonly used for comparison. As with sentence stems, a major challenge of using Venn diagrams is the necessity of guiding students in identifying differences that are related to the same characteristic. To help meet this challenge, you can use a modified Venn diagram that includes pairs of differences, with each set assigned a number so students see that each pair of differences must relate to a common characteristic. (See Appendix A for a template you can use as a blackline master.)

In Figure 4.1, you can see that the paired differences focus on general characteristics of the two terms.

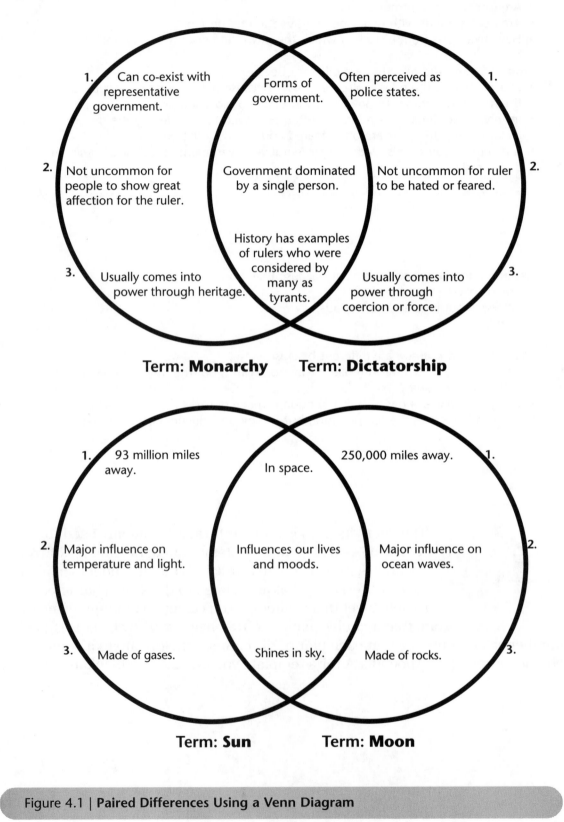

**Term: Monarchy**   **Term: Dictatorship**

1. Can co-exist with representative government.

2. Not uncommon for people to show great affection for the ruler.

3. Usually comes into power through heritage.

Forms of government.

Government dominated by a single person.

History has examples of rulers who were considered by many as tyrants.

1. Often perceived as police states.

2. Not uncommon for ruler to be hated or feared.

3. Usually comes into power through coercion or force.

**Term: Sun**   **Term: Moon**

1. 93 million miles away.

2. Major influence on temperature and light.

3. Made of gases.

In space.

Influences our lives and moods.

Shines in sky.

1. 250,000 miles away.

2. Major influence on ocean waves.

3. Made of rocks.

**Figure 4.1 | Paired Differences Using a Venn Diagram**

**Double Bubble**

David Hyerle, in his book *Visual Tools for Constructing Knowledge*, recommends and illustrates the use of the double bubble to format comparisons. The basic format is shown in Figure 4.2.

Students identify the two items they are going to compare and then record the information in the appropriate bubbles. Consistent with the above recommendations for using Venn diagrams, it is suggested that students number the "differences" bubbles to ensure that they focus on general characteristics of the items. Figure 4.3 shows an example. (See Appendix A for a template you can use as a blackline master.)

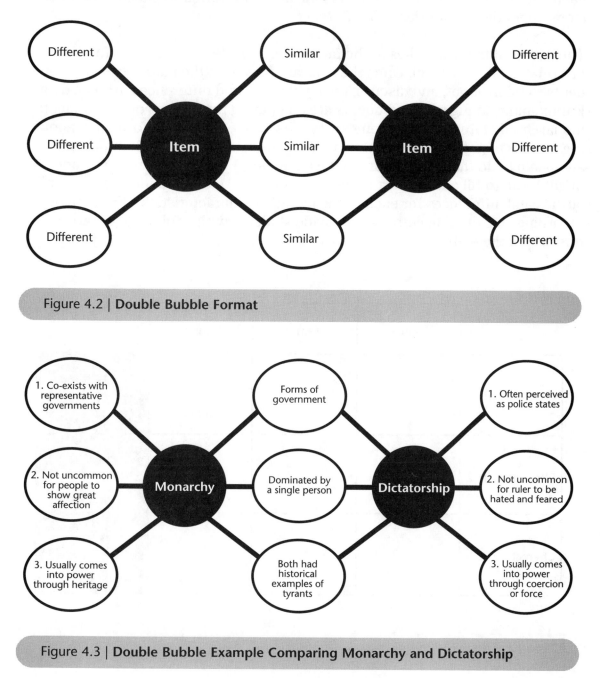

Figure 4.2 | **Double Bubble Format**

Figure 4.3 | **Double Bubble Example Comparing Monarchy and Dictatorship**

**Matrix**

The final comparison format we'll look at is the matrix, shown in Figure 4.4.

In the column headings, students place the terms they are going to compare. Notice that the matrix, unlike the other formats discussed in this chapter, lends itself to comparing more than two terms at a time. In the rows, the students identify the general characteristics on which they will base their comparison. In the cells, they briefly describe each term as it relates to each characteristic. Finally, students look at their information and draw conclusions about the similarities and differences.

The power of the matrix lies in the fact that it provides an organizer for the information about a term. Once the cells are filled out, the matrix can guide students to think about, and discuss, the similarities and differences in some detail. For example, in Figure 4.5, students are comparing three types of government: monarchy, dictatorship, and democracy. First, they fill in the information about these types of government, as shown. Next, students review their information and begin to do the comparison. In the example, you can also see how students might begin to fill out the part of the matrix that asks them to identify the similarities and differences for each of the identified characteristics. (For ease of recording, it is often necessary to provide students with a full-page version of this part of the matrix.)

|  | Item 1 | Item 2 | Item 3 |  |
|---|---|---|---|---|
| **Characteristic 1** |  |  |  | **Similarities & Differences** |
| **Characteristic 2** |  |  |  | **Similarities & Differences** |
| **Characteristic 3** |  |  |  | **Similarities & Differences** |

Figure 4.4 | **Matrix Format**

| | Monarchy | Dictatorship | Democracy | Similarities & Differences |
|---|---|---|---|---|
| **How the leaders come to power** | King or queen gains throne out of heritage. Sometimes a monarch takes over country by force. Often a leader for life. | The dictator usually takes power through coercion or force. Often is leader for life. | Leaders are elected by the people, sometimes influenced by others. The leader doesn't have total power. Maybe voted out of office. | Actually, monarchy and dictatorship are more alike and democracy is different. Monarchs and dictatorships are similar in that power over people is taken by, or given to, an individual, but in a democracy, the people decide who will have the power. Even though monarchy and dictatorship are somewhat similar, they are also different in that the dictator takes over by force, but the monarch is usually designated as a result of heritage. |
| **The reaction from the people** | Throughout history are examples of monarchs loved by the people, but some were hated by certain persecuted groups. | Often in history the dictator is hated or feared by most people. | People are often split on their reactions but accept the elected leader, knowing they can try to elect a new one before too long. | Similarities & Differences |
| **The role of the people** | People are generally expected to obey the rule of the monarch. Monarch holds power and can change laws. Can become like dictators. | People must obey the dictator. Often there are serious consequences to not being loyal. | Generally the people are seen to have power through their votes. If they don't like what's happening, they can elect new leaders. | Similarities & Differences |

Figure 4.5 | **Matrix Example Comparing Monarchy, Dictatorship, and Democacy**

Individual students can use the matrix, but it is also can be a vehicle for encouraging students in a small group to engage in robust conversations about what they see as similarities and differences. Often, these conversations result in students revising and adding information in the cells, or even adding another row or column to the matrix. (See Appendix A for a template you can use as a blackline master.)

## Procedure

Present students with, or have them identify, terms from their notebooks to compare. Allow them to work in small groups and give them a few minutes to distinguish similarities and differences and to record their ideas in one of the four formats: sentence stems, Venn diagram, double bubble, or matrix. Ask them to share their ideas aloud. At various points during this sharing time, and at the end, encourage students to make additions and revisions to their entries for the targeted terms. Monitor their work to ensure that their additions and revisions are accurate.

**Tip:** If, initially, students identify only the most obvious similarities and differences, provide a few more minutes for them to work in their groups. Challenge them to identify additional interesting and meaningful similarities and differences.

# Classifying Terms

## Description

Classifying is a process of grouping on the basis of similar attributes. Creating categories and then placing terms into the categories requires students to identify key attributes of concepts associated with the terms, and to have sufficient understanding of those attributes to recognize them in other terms.

Classification tasks can be either structured or open-ended. In structured tasks, students are given the terms to classify and the categories into which they must place them. For example, they might classify a list of conflicts in history according to their major causes: economic, social, or political.

A more open-ended task would provide either the list of terms to classify or the categories, but not both. For example, students might be given the following terms to classify: *plateau, mesa, mountain, bay, ocean, canyon, hill, glen, forest, plain, port, canal, reservoir, stream,* and *prairie.* Students might decide to classify them based on the type of topography, according to their size, or whether they are natural or manmade. They could even be asked to add other terms to their categories.

The most open-ended task would allow students to identify what they are classifying *and* the categories into which they will classify them.

## Procedure

Set up classifying tasks for students in any of the following ways:

- Give students a list of terms from their notebooks and ask them to classify the terms. The terms might be related, such as a list of bodies of water, or they might be unrelated, thus requiring students to think creatively to form categories. For example, you might ask them to classify the following terms: *urban, fraction, The Odyssey, rhythm, cardiac, supply, demand, mammal, equation,* and *mutualism.*

- Create categories for students and ask them to find terms from their notebooks that might fit into those categories. For example, ask them to identify people in history who were known for what they did for others or were known for caring more about themselves than about others.

- Ask students to review all of the terms in a particular section of their notebooks—for example, all of their math terms. Challenge them to create their own categories for those terms and classify as many terms as possible.

Allow students to work in pairs or small groups to complete classifying tasks. After they have had time to work, invite several groups to share their ideas. Make sure that they are able to explain the following:

- The criteria for membership in a category.

- The items they included in each category.

- How each item meets the criteria for placement in a category.

**Tip:** If time allows, ask students to reclassify their terms with new categories. Students do some of their best thinking when they are challenged to classify, and then *reclassify*, the same list of items.

# Solving Analogy Problems

**Review Activity**

## Description

A complete analogy contains two terms in the first set (A and B) that have the same relationship as the two terms in the second set (C and D). A common format for an analogy statement is as follows:

*A* is to *B* as *C* is to *D*.

In analogy problems, one or two terms are missing and students must complete the statement by providing terms that will complete the analogy.

If only one term is missing, the field of possible accurate answers is narrowed considerably. Examples include the following:

*Bone* is to *skeleton* as *word* is to _____.

*Inch* is to *foot* as *millimeter* is to _____.

*Martin Luther King Jr.* is to *civil rights* as _____ is to *women's rights*.

When two terms are missing, an analogy can be completed with a wider variety of answers. In the examples below, many different perspectives can be applied to complete the analogies.

*Harry Truman* is to *World War II* as _____ is to _____.

*Rhythm* is to *music* as _____ is to _____.

*Bury My Heart at Wounded Knee* is to *Native Americans* as _____ is to _____.

## Procedure

Present students with analogy problems, using either an oral or written format, and give them the opportunity to provide the missing terms. Allow students to work in pairs or small groups so they can discuss their ideas with one another.

Invite students to share their answers aloud. As they share, make sure that they include a description of the *relationship* that both sets of terms have in common. In the first example of analogy problems with one missing term, students would explain that a bone is *part of* a skeleton; thus, the first item in the second part of the sentence (a word) must be *part of* whatever answer they provide as the second item.

One way to help students understand analogies is to use a graphic organizer that has space for the relationship to be written. Figure 4.6 is adapted from David Hyerle's book *Visual Tools for Constructing Knowledge* (1996).

Notice that on the bottom line, students write what Hyerle refers to as the "relating factor." This format helps to highlight the importance of being clear about *how* the items in each set are related. See Appendix A for a blackline master of this analogy organizer.

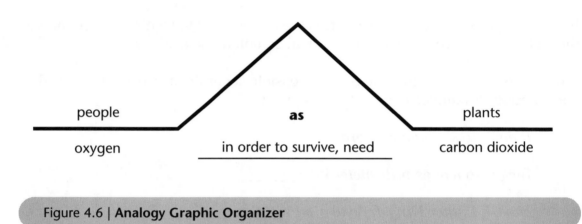

| people | as | plants |
|--------|-----|--------|
| oxygen | in order to survive, need | carbon dioxide |

**Figure 4.6 | Analogy Graphic Organizer**

- - - - - - - - - - - - - - - - - - - - - - - - - - - - - - - - - - - - - - - - - - -

**Tips:** Analogy problems with two missing terms provide opportunities for students to think beyond the obvious relationships, thereby helping them to gain new insights into the analogy terms. The Harry Truman sentence on the previous page, for example, provides multiple ways to describe the relationship between Truman and World War II. Students could write that Harry Truman *could have prevented* World War II or that Harry Truman *is known for his leadership during* World War II. The only requirement should be that students identify and explain the relationship between the first two items and then apply that relationship accurately to the second set of items.

Although the focus should be on the terms in their notebooks, you might increase students' engagement by occasionally including in the analogy problems some "everyday" terms not found in their notebooks. For example, ask students to complete the following: *Rhythm* is to *music* as _____ is to *skateboarding.*

You can engage students in even more open-ended tasks by asking them to create and explain original analogies. Keep in mind, however, that most students will first need multiple experiences with teacher-prepared analogy problems like the ones in the examples.

# Creating Metaphors

**Review Activity**

## Description

Metaphors expose how objects or ideas that seem quite different might actually be, at a more general level, very similar. A classic example of metaphorical thinking is the statement, "Love is a rose." The concepts *love* and *rose*, taken literally, are very different. However, they have general attributes in common; for example, they both have qualities that attract people, and they both can cause pain.

The goal of this activity is not necessarily to have students create poetic metaphors, although that is possible, but rather to guide them to see general relationships among terms in their notebooks or between a term and another seemingly different idea.

## Procedure

To engage students in metaphorical thinking, model the process and give explicit guidance. Follow some simple, concrete steps, such as the following:

**Step 1:** List the specific characteristics of a targeted term.

**Step 2:** Rewrite those characteristics in more general language.

**Step 3:** Identify another specific term and explain how it also has the general characteristics identified during Step 2.

Creating a matrix can help students complete these steps. In Figure 4.7, students have been guided through the first two steps and are now asked to identify someone who might be considered the "Frederick Douglass" for another era or another cause. In this example, the student is going to show how Helen Keller shared characteristics with Douglass.

As another example, if students were examining the term *labor union*, the first two steps might include the information in Figure 4.8.

Step 3 requires students to think of other specific examples of situations that have the same general pattern as that articulated in Step 2. For example, students might identify the civil rights movement or the women's movement, or they might see how the general pattern describes revolutions in history, the growth of political parties, or the plot of a story they have read.

| Term | More General Description | Term |
|---|---|---|
| *Frederick Douglass* | | *Helen Keller* |
| Was a slave as a young boy. | Had a rough beginning. | Got sick as a baby, which left her deaf and blind. |
| Learned to read and write anyway. | Achieved goals even when difficult. | Learned how to read Braille, write; she also went to college. |
| Wrote books and gave speeches against slavery. | Worked to help other people who suffered like him. | Through her speech tours and writing, she inspired others to overcome their disabilities. |

Figure 4.7 | **Metaphor Matrix Example to Probe Similarities**

| Term | More General Description | Term |
|---|---|---|
| *Labor Unions* | | *?* |
| Unions were formed when workers felt that employers were not providing fair wages, safe conditions, and reasonable hours. | Workers united because powerful others were treating them unfairly. | |
| When many workers joined, the unions began to have the power to demand better conditions. | As the united group grew, it became powerful enough to improve working conditions. | |
| Sometimes workers who did not join experienced anger and even violence toward them from members. | Those who would not join in with this new group were treated poorly by the group members. | |

Figure 4.8 | **Partial Metaphor Matrix Example**

**Tip:** At first, students might need significant guidance and modeling for this activity, especially as they try to decide just how general the language in Step 2 should be. Interestingly, however, teachers who use this process report that students who struggle with assignments requiring extensive writing sometimes demonstrate deep levels of insight when the focus is on this type of thinking. Set up small-group and whole-class interactions to provide opportunities for these students to shine.

# Games for Step 6

Step 6 of the six-step teaching process suggests that games can provide opportunities to review terms as well as interject an energizing break into the routine of the day. The nature and structure of the games described in this section allow you to use them in a scheduled block of time for review, at the beginning or end of a lesson, or as the first activity in the morning and the last activity in the afternoon. You can also use the games to energize students any time they seem lethargic or inattentive. As energizers, the games frequently help students become more alert and willing to learn. Unlike simple physical energizers, the games described here have the added benefit of enhancing students' understanding of terms important to their academic success.

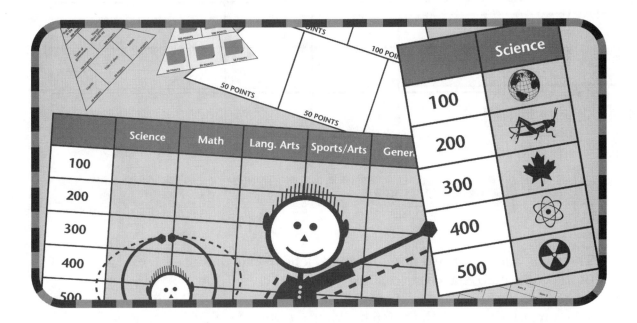

**Game Activity**

# What Is the Question?

## Description

This game is modeled after the popular television show *Jeopardy!* It requires a simple game matrix (see Figure 4.9), which can be created on an overhead transparency or a white board, or as a slide using PowerPoint or other presentation software. (See Appendix A for a template you can use as a blackline master.)

|     | Science | Math | Lang. Arts | Sports/Arts | General |
|-----|---------|------|------------|-------------|---------|
| **100** |     |      |            |             |         |
| **200** |     |      |            |             |         |
| **300** |     |      |            |             |         |
| **400** |     |      |            |             |         |
| **500** |     |      |            |             |         |

Figure 4.9 | **What Is the Question Matrix**

The game allows for two possible approaches—one that uses *words* in the cells of the game matrix and one that uses *pictures*.

When words are used, the teacher writes a term in each cell (see Figure 4.10), then covers the cell with a sticky note or hides the term using software animation. As the teacher reveals each term, students indicate that they know the meaning by stating a question for which the term would be the answer.

For example, for the hidden term "earthquake," several questions would be acceptable, including "What is measured on a Richter scale?" or "What do people in California fear will happen because of the San Andreas Fault?" For the hidden term "O. Henry," students could reply, "Who wrote 'The Cop and the Anthem'?" or "What writer was known for surprise endings?"

|  | Science | Math | Lang. Arts | Sports/Arts | General |
|---|---|---|---|---|---|
| **100** | Earthquake | Fraction | Adverb | Mona Lisa | Peanut Butter |
| **200** | Precipitation | Decimal | Setting | Love-Love | Marshmallow |
| **300** | Photosynthesis | Parallel | Antonym | Van Gogh | James Bond |
| **400** | Gravity | Equation | "Nevermore" | Cardiovascular | Walt Disney |
| **500** | Decibel | Hypotenuse | Maya Angelou | Impressionist | Jaguar |

Figure 4.10 | **What Is the Question Matrix with Words**

The teacher decides whether a student's question represents an adequate understanding of the term. For example, if a student said, "What makes you nervous?" for the term "earthquake," the teacher might respond that the question doesn't adequately demonstrate an understanding of an important feature of earthquakes.

Notice that in Figure 4.10, the last column exists mainly for fun. Although the focus of this game is on terms important to academic content, including some general, fun items in the last column will help keep students' attention.

Playing the game with pictures instead of words requires more preparation, because pictures must be found or created for each cell. This can be done with clip art (when using a software presentation program), drawings (when using overhead transparencies), or with a combination of photos and drawings (when using a white board). As the teacher reveals each picture, students form a question that demonstrates they recognize the picture. An example of what might appear in a science column is shown in Figure 4.11. In the 200-point cell, the teacher would be looking for a question such as "What is an insect?"

## Procedure

Prepare the game board matrix ahead of time and hide the cell contents as described above.

Place the students in teams or pairs. Select, or let the students select, a team leader who will raise her hand and provide the answer that the team agrees

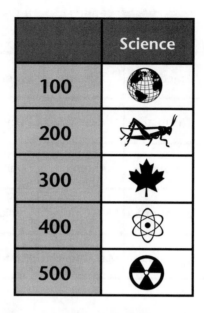

| | Science |
|---|---|
| 100 | 🌐 |
| 200 | 🦗 |
| 300 | 🍁 |
| 400 | ⚛ |
| 500 | ☢ |

**Figure 4.11 | What Is the Question Matrix with Pictures**

upon. You need to decide whether to give each team a turn in sequence or to call on whichever team indicates they know the answer first. This latter approach can be fun and encourage friendly competition, but it is sometimes difficult to determine who raised their hand first.

If the team leader called upon provides a correct answer (i.e., question), that team gets the points. If the answer is incorrect, the team gets no points and another team gets a chance to provide an answer.

**Tip:** Scoring and calling on teams can be organized in a variety of ways; students will have suggestions for doing this. You might find, however, that students have about as much fun, and are equally engaged, when they simply try to guess the answers without actually keeping score.

Game Activity

# Vocabulary Charades

## Description

This game, particularly energizing because it involves movement, is named after the popular parlor game that requires players to silently act out ideas. You can take two approaches to playing this game in the classroom. In the first, students simply stand next to their desks and use their arms, legs, and bodies to show they know the meaning of each term called out by the teacher. For example, in response to *radius, diameter,* and *circumference*, students might position themselves as shown in Figure 4.12.

Figure 4.12 | **Vocabulary Charades for *Radius, Diameter,* and *Circumference.***

In the second approach, students form teams and then give designated team members a term to act out. The other team members must guess the term as quickly as possible. With this approach, you can set the game up as a competition among teams or as a competition in which teams simply try to beat their previous record.

## Procedure

You can use the first approach, which takes only a few minutes or even seconds, periodically throughout a day or a lesson. Ask students to stand up next to their desks. Explain that you are going to call out several terms and that their challenge is to show that they know the meaning of each term by taking a position or acting the term out using their arms, legs, and bodies without speaking. Use the examples of *radius, diameter,* and *circumference* as described previously. Other terms might require students to act out a little scene or interact with someone.

As you say each term, give students time to figure out how to show the meaning. With terms you have used before, students will probably be very quick in their responses. A new term, especially one that is abstract, may require more time. When you are satisfied that students are accurately depicting the meaning of the term, call out a new term. You might use only terms related to a single topic, or you might use terms from different topics or different subject areas.

With the second approach, organize students into teams. (You may want to establish teams that stay together over a period of time so that you will not have to create teams each time you play this game.) Create—or have students create—decks of index cards, each containing one term. If several teams are going to play simultaneously, prepare several identical decks so that each team can hold the cards with the terms they are acting out.

To play the game, give one or more cards to each team member designated as the "actor." Instruct the actors to stand in front of their teams and begin to act out the term or terms. Establish a way for the actors to communicate—without talking—that the team has, indeed, guessed the term. For example, allow the actor to show the team the card as a cue that they have guessed correctly. Because students become quite effective and quick at guessing the terms, you will probably want to include several terms for the actors in each round of the game.

- - - - - - - - - - - - - - - - - - - - - - - - - - - - - - - - - - - - - - - - -

**Tip:** You can play this game in several ways. You can have one team at a time play the game while the other teams watch, or you can have teams play simultaneously. You can set up a competition or simply let students play for fun. Teachers report that all of these approaches work well and that students often come up with creative variations on the rules.

**Game
Activity**

# Name That Category

## Description

This engaging game, modeled after the television show *The $100,000 Pyramid*, helps students focus on the attributes of concepts represented by or associated with terms as they try to determine what the terms in a list have in common.

In this example, we use a game board in the shape of a triangle, similar to the one used on the television show (see Figure 4.13), but the board can be any shape. (See Appendix A for a template you can use as a blackline master.)

The object of the game is for a clue giver, who sees one category at a time on the game board, to list words that fit that category until teammates correctly identify the category name.

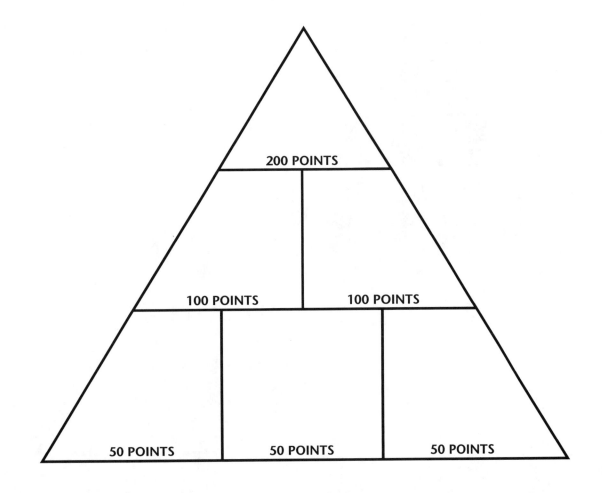

Figure 4.13 | **Name That Category Game Board**

## Procedure

Decide on a shape for the game board and then create a permanent template on an overhead transparency, on a white board, or using computer presentation software, such as PowerPoint.

Each time you prepare the game, write a category name within each cell, ideally increasing the level of difficulty as you move through the categories. At the beginning of each round of the game, hide the category names, perhaps with sticky notes (see Figure 4.14). If PowerPoint or another software program is used, hide the categories using the features of the software.

To play the game, assign students to work in pairs or small groups. Be certain that one player on each team, the clue giver, can see the game board. Require the others, the guessers, to keep their backs to the board or screen.

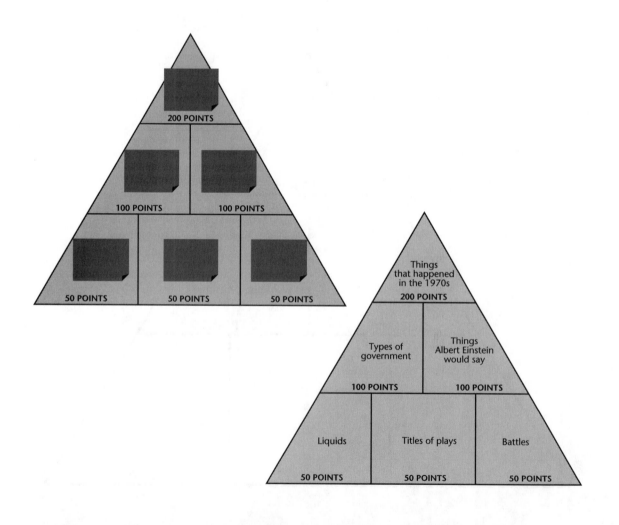

Figure 4.14 | **Covered and Uncovered Game Boards**

As you reveal the first category, tell the clue giver to begin to list terms that pertain to that category. For example, for the first category shown at the bottom of Figure 4.14, the clue giver might say, "water, milk, soda, tea, coffee . . ." and keep listing terms until the guessers name the category—in this case, "liquids."

Reveal the next category as soon as you see that a team has correctly identified the first category and is ready to move to the next. Remind the clue givers to check the board to see whether the next category name has been revealed, and, if it has, to begin to list items in that category. Tell clue givers that if their team is ready for a new category but they check the board and find that the next category is still covered, they should yell, "Go!" to get your attention so you will know a team is ready to move on. Explain to the clue givers that when their teams have guessed all the categories, they should raise their hands and shout, "Got it!" This is the cue for all teams to stop. Award all teams the number of points they have earned up to that time. If you continue the game with another round, designate new clue givers.

**Tips:** Although the directions above suggest that the clue giver "shout," you can certainly come up with other, more subdued cues, especially if you have a large or particularly excitable class.

After each round, take time to have several students share some of the items they included in their lists, highlighting those items that were particularly helpful to their team in identifying the category name.

You can engage students in this game in a variety of ways: You can keep track of points, or just play for fun. Instead of setting up the game as a competition, you can let teams try to beat their own previously recorded time. You can even let students help you design variations on the rules and format.

**Game Activity**

# Draw Me

## Description

This game is modeled after the popular game *Pictionary,* which requires players to draw pictures as clues to help teammates identify a particular term. Playing this game in the classroom helps students attach images to word meanings.

Those familiar with *Pictionary* know that one team member draws pictures in order to elicit a word or phrase from the team. To adapt the game to classroom use, for each round, have students draw pictures representing several words belonging to a cluster of related words. For example, a student might be asked to draw pictures representing *inch, foot, yard,* and *mile;* or *United States, Canada, England,* and *India;* or *oxygen, carbon dioxide, helium,* and *neon.* This not only engages students in attaching images to words but also helps them review several words during one round of play.

Even though most students like playing this game, two types of problems sometimes surface. First, some students may resist playing because they claim that they "can't draw." After seeing others' drawings and playing the game themselves, their resistance usually dissipates and they realize that the goal is to represent ideas, not to create art. Students soon understand that a picture like the one in Figure 4.15 may not be well drawn, but it still conveys the idea of the United States.

Second, some students may resist because they *like* to create art and, therefore, try to draw masterpieces for the terms. The result is that they, and their teammates, do not do well. After playing several times, these students typically realize

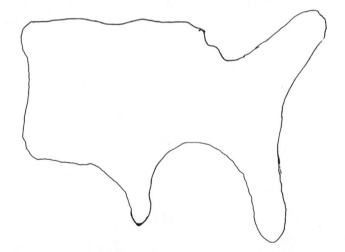

Figure 4.15 | **Draw Me Example**

that their team will fare better in the game if they abandon the colored pencils and fancy borders and, instead, create rough representations of word meanings.

## Procedure

Organize students to work in pairs or small groups, with one student per team designated as the one who draws. (Ideally, try to allow time to play enough rounds that all members of each group have the opportunity to draw; if time is limited, have the students play the game in pairs.) Be sure that the person doing the drawing faces the word display and that the teammates doing the guessing have their backs to the display.

Using an overhead projector, a white board, or presentation software, display a cluster of terms—usually three or four—and say, "Go!" The designated "drawers" are to draw pictures representing the meaning of the terms, using no letters or numbers, until the team guesses all of the words in the cluster. When the team has guessed all of the words, tell the drawer to raise his hand or say, "Got it!" At that point, tell all teams to stop drawing. Award the winning team a point. Then designate a new drawer for each team and begin the next round with a new set of terms.

**Tips:** After each round, encourage teams to examine other teams' drawings. In this way, students will have a chance to see a number of different pictorial renderings of the words and will be able to enhance and revise their own mental images of the terms.

Develop with students some hints for quick imaging. For example, everyone in the class can agree that if a picture of a person is needed, the drawing usually does not need to include legs and arms. For example a variety of quick depictions are shown in Figure 4.16.

These types of tips not only will enhance students' ability to play the game but also can help them become more skilled at creating meaningful images in their vocabulary notebooks.

Figure 4.16 | Basic "Person" Drawings

**Game Activity**

# Talk a Mile a Minute

## Description

In this game, teams of students are given a list of terms that have been organized into categories. Typically, the words in the list are related by meaning, such as "parts of a circle," or "things associated with the planets." Occasionally, however, the list could be organized differently—for example, to include words that begin with a particular letter. This format, although more difficult for students, allows for clustering words from different disciplines.

To play each round, every team designates a "talker" who is provided with a list of words under a category title, such as the list in the following example.

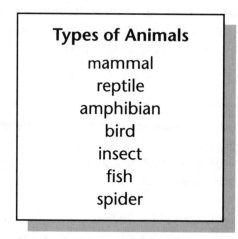

**Types of Animals**

mammal
reptile
amphibian
bird
insect
fish
spider

The talker tries to get the team to say each of the words by quickly describing them. The talker is allowed to say anything about the terms, "talking a mile a minute," but may not use any words in the category title or any rhyming words. In the list above, for example, the talker must not say the word *animal* when giving the clues. For the word *mammal*, the talker might say something like, "These are living things that give birth to live young. Examples are dogs, horses, and monkeys."

The talker keeps talking until the team members identify the first term in the category. The talker then moves quickly to the next term in the category until all terms have been guessed or time has been called.

Additional examples of categories and terms are shown in Figure 4.17.

**Things Associated with the American Civil War**

Robert E. Lee
Ulysses S. Grant
Gettysburg
Slavery
Antietam
Emancipation Proclamation
Abraham Lincoln

**Things Associated with Outer Space**

Sun
Orbits
Mars
Venus
Saturn
Galaxy
Meteors

**Shapes**

Square
Circle
Rectangle
Triangle
Right Triangle
Oval
Diamond

**Artists**

Vincent Van Gogh
Michelangelo
Picasso
Leonardo da Vinci
Monet
Rembrandt
Andy Warhol

**Units of Measure**

Inches
Meters
Gallons
Hours
Quarts
Square Yards
Liters

**Parts of Speech**

Noun
Verb
Adjective
Preposition
Conjunction
Adverb
Pronoun

Figure 4.17 | **Talk a Mile a Minute Sample Categories and Terms**

## Procedure

Arrange students to work in pairs or small groups, with one student per group designated as the talker. (Ideally, allow time for enough rounds, or categories, to give everyone an opportunity to be the talker; if time is limited, have the students play the game in pairs.) Decide whether you want to play the game with many teams working simultaneously, or give each team a turn in sequence. If you are playing with multiple teams working simultaneously, be sure the talker for each team gets a card with the words or is facing the area where you have chosen to display the terms. (You may choose to display them on an overhead transparency, white board, or screen using presentation software.) Be sure that the other team members—the guessers—have their backs to the display.

Give the talkers a signal to begin giving clues. When one minute is up, tell all teams to stop and to count their points, one point for each term they guessed. If a team finishes before the minute is up and the talker yells, "Got it," tell all teams to stop and count the points they accumulated (one per correctly identified term) before time was called.

**Tips:** You can keep score and give prizes or simply let students play the game for fun without assigning points.

You can tie the game into a math or art activity in which students review shapes, dimensions, or principles of design and then create game cards. Students are often very good at creating game cards.

# Reference

Hyerle, D. (1996). *Visual tools for constructing knowledge*. Alexandria, VA: Association for Supervision and Curriculum Development.

# 5 | Managing the Program

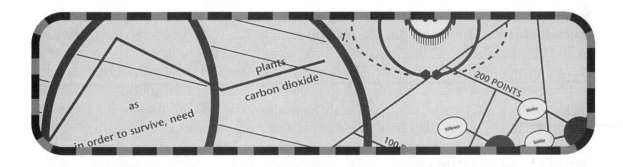

Although the concept of building academic background knowledge through direct vocabulary instruction is simple and straightforward, putting such a program into practice requires effective management of at least three elements: (1) the student notebooks, (2) the terms in the appendix of each student notebook that are not taught directly, and (3) the time needed to implement the program adequately.

## The Student Notebook

The student notebook is a central feature of this program. The appendix of each student notebook contains all of the terms at all levels within 11 subject areas. To recall the format of the pages in the student notebook, reexamine Figure 3.1 in Chapter 3.

It is probably safe to say that no school or district will teach terms from every subject area for any of the four levels. More likely, a school or district will select terms from four or five subject areas, such as language arts, mathematics, science, history, and physical education. As Chapter 2 describes, even within a given subject area, only some of the terms will be selected for direct instruction.

Each page of the student notebook includes room in the border where the subject area can be recorded (see Figure 3.1). Pages can also be color-coded so that students can easily identify the different subject areas. For example, you might decide that all mathematics terms will be recorded on blue pages, all language arts terms on red pages, and so on.

Also in Figure 3.1, note the space at the bottom of each page. If you want your students to keep their notebooks in approximate alphabetical order, you might have them record the initial letter of each term at the bottom of the page. For example, a mathematics teacher who introduces the terms *mean* and *median* in the same week might ask students to record both terms on a single page and to write the letter *M* at the bottom of the page. The students would then place that page in the mathematics section of the notebook among other pages for terms beginning with the letter *M*.

Another option is to organize terms by unit, theme, or topic. For example, a science teacher conducting a unit on habitats might have students record the word *habitat* in the border at the bottom of the page. All terms taught in the context of the unit would have the word *habitat* at the bottom of their respective pages, and these pages would all be placed together in the student notebook. Organizing terms by unit, theme, or topic facilitates many of the activities and games described in Chapter 4, such as those involving comparison and classification.

One of the most useful features of the student notebook is that it can be used from one year to the next. As depicted in Figure 2.1, Level 2 (grades 3–5) has 190 mathematics terms. Assuming that 30 terms are taught each year for all three years, 90 of the 190 terms could be addressed over that period. Students in a school might turn in their notebooks at the end of one school year and pick them up again at the beginning of the next. During the subsequent year, students would add terms to those recorded the previous year. In this way, each student's notebook would become a growing document reflecting the student's deepening and expanding understanding of a subject area over several years.

## Managing the Terms That Are Not Taught Directly

As we noted earlier, it is unlikely that a school would teach terms from all 11 subject areas every year. Even within a given subject area for which terms *are* taught, all terms probably won't be addressed. What, then, should be done with the terms in the appendix of a student notebook that are not taught?

We highly recommend having a section in each notebook for students to record terms that they select to learn on their own. They might choose terms from the appendix of their notebooks or from their personal reading or both. Also note that students have access to all terms at all levels for the 11 subject areas. Even though many of these terms might be quite sophisticated, especially for younger students, providing all terms at all levels gives students a sense of the scope of subject matter terminology.

Ideally, providing students with all 7,923 terms will inspire and encourage them to study and learn basic and advanced terminology in subject areas that are of interest to them but that might not be formally taught in their school. For example, an elementary school might not teach any of the technology terms listed in the appendix. However, interested students in grades 3–5 might create their own personal technology sections in their notebooks and select words to learn on their own that come from their own grade-level interval or higher grade-level intervals. A list of terms selected by a particular 4th grade student might include: *software piracy, virus, modem, network, malfunction, byte, megabyte,* and *streaming,* to name a few. Finally, the comprehensive list of terms in all 11 subject areas might capture the attention and imagination of parents. Parents and children might informally select terms from subject areas not directly addressed in school and discuss their meanings and use.

## Managing Time

Without question, the approach described in this manual requires a time commitment. Specifically, each teacher in the subject areas for which terms will be taught must agree to spend enough time each week to teach the target terms adequately.

If a school keeps the number of target terms within each subject area small, the teachers' responsibility to teach them should not be a burden. For example, teaching one, two, or even three terms per week for 30 weeks in a given subject area does not require an inordinate amount of time. Also, because most subject-matter teachers include vocabulary in their instructional practice, teaching one, two, or three target words per week should fit right into regular classroom routines. However, at least three aspects of the six-step process described in Chapter 3 do require extra time.

First, teachers must set aside time periodically to engage students in activities that help them add to their knowledge base (see Step 4 described in Chapter 3). Many of these activities were described in some depth in Chapter 4, including free association, comparing, classifying, solving analogy problems, and creating metaphors. By definition, these activities help students think about academic terms and phrases in new and deeper ways. In Chapter 3, we recommended that students be allowed to add to the information in their notebooks after these activities.

Second, teachers must set aside time to allow students to discuss the terms with one another (see Step 5 described in Chapter 3). Although this can be accomplished in many ways, we described a Think-Pair-Share activity. Again, it was recommended that students be encouraged to add to the information in their notebooks after they have discussed terms with one another.

We recommend that teachers set aside at least one 15- to 20-minute period per week for either Step 4 or Step 5 activities. For example, one week a teacher might engage students in a comparison activity with selected terms (Step 4). At the end of that activity, students would be given some time to add information to their notebooks for the terms covered in the comparison activity. The next week, students might engage in a Think-Pair-Share activity, after which they would again be given time to add relevant information to their notebooks. Thus, each week, students would have at least one 15- to 20-minute period to interact with the terms that have been taught using Steps 1, 2, and 3 of the process for teaching academic terms in such a way as to sharpen and add to their understanding of those terms.

Third, teachers must set aside time periodically for students to play games with the terms in their notebooks (see Step 6 described in Chapter 3). Many of these games were described in Chapter 4. We recommend that these games be played at least three times every two weeks. Games should be played at times in the day when students' energy typically runs low or their attention wanes. The games will provide students with an informal review of the terms they have been studying, help generate energy, and focus students' attention for other academic activities.

In terms of Steps 4, 5, and 6, then, a typical two-week period might resemble that depicted in Figure 5.1.

| Monday | Tuesday | Wednesday | Thursday | Friday |
|--------|---------|-----------|----------|--------|
|        | Vocabulary game played right before lunch period. (Step 6) |           | Comparison Activity (Step 4) | Vocabulary game played at the end of the day. (Step 6) |
| Monday | Tuesday | Wednesday | Thursday | Friday |
|        | Vocabulary game played right before lunch. (Step 6) |           | Think-Pair-Share Activity (Step 5) |        |

Figure 5.1 | **Minimum Expectations for Use of Steps 4, 5, and 6 in a Typical Two-Week Period**

In summary, the amount of time required to implement the program described in this manual is significant but not inordinate. We believe that if a school as a whole and the individual teachers in the school are willing to examine their current practice, they can find time to implement the program, perhaps by eliminating some current activities that might not contribute as much to student learning.

# Final Thoughts

The influence of academic background knowledge on academic achievement is fully and firmly documented in research. It stands to reason, then, that enhancing students' background knowledge would be one sure, strong way to improve students' academic performance and narrow the achievement gap. As stated in *Building Background Knowledge for Academic Achievement,* "Enhancing students' academic background knowledge . . . is a worthy goal of public education from a number of perspectives. In fact, given the relationship between academic background knowledge and academic achievement, one can make the case that it should be at the top of any list of interventions intended to enhance student achievement" (p. 4).

In this manual, we have proposed just such an intervention. We have described a program to enhance the academic background knowledge of students via direct instruction in subject-matter terms.

Through a brief review of the research, we have explained why a comprehensive vocabulary instruction program is needed and how its successful implementation can make a significant difference for students. We have provided a list of 7,923 academic terms, culled from national standards documents, across 11 subject areas from kindergarten through grade 12. We have defined a method by which individual teachers, single-school faculties, or entire school systems can select, organize, and customize lists of terms for each grade level. We have provided a template for pages in a student notebook that could be used from year to year. We have suggested a six-step process for teaching the academic terms, as well as a variety of strategies to review and reinforce the terms throughout the school year. Finally, we have offered ideas for managing the program and the time it would require.

We believe that teachers, schools, and districts that embrace the comprehensive approach taken by the program we have described will see impressive results in classrooms and on achievement tests. More important, we believe the program can leave a powerful and lasting imprint on students and their learning.

# About the Authors

**Robert J. Marzano** is a senior scholar at Mid-continent Research for Education and Learning in Aurora, Colorado; an associate professor at Cardinal Stritch University in Milwaukee, Wisconsin; vice president of Pathfinder Education, Inc.; and president of Marzano & Associates consulting firm in Centennial, Colorado. He has developed programs and practices used in K–12 classrooms that translate current research and theory in cognition into instructional methods. An internationally known trainer and speaker, Marzano has authored 20 books and more than 150 articles and chapters on topics such as reading and writing instruction, thinking skills, school effectiveness, restructuring, assessment, cognition, and standards implementation. Recent ASCD titles include *Building Background Knowledge for Academic Achievement: Research on What Works in Schools* (2004); *Classroom Management That Works: Research Based Strategies for Every Teacher* (Marzano, Marzano, & Pickering, 2003); *What Works in Schools: Translating Research into Action* (2003); *A Handbook for Classroom Instruction That Works* (Marzano, Paynter, Pickering, & Gaddy, 2001); and *Classroom Instruction That Works: Research-Based Strategies for Increasing Student Achievement* (Marzano, Pickering, & Pollack, 2001). Additionally, Marzano headed a team of authors who developed *Dimensions of Learning* (ASCD, 1992). Most recently, he contributed to *Building Academic Background Knowledge: Facilitator's Guide* (2005). Marzano received his bachelor's degree in English from Iona College in New York, a master's degree in reading/language arts from Seattle University, and a doctorate in curriculum and instruction from the University of Washington. He can be contacted at 7127 South Danube Court, Centennial, CO 80016. Phone: 1-303-796-7683. E-mail: robertjmarzano@aol.com.

**Debra J. Pickering** is a private consultant and director of staff development in Littleton Public Schools, Littleton, Colorado. During more than 25 years in education, she has gained practical experience as a classroom teacher and district staff development coordinator and has done extensive consulting with administrators and teachers, K–12. Her work in research and development centers on the study of learning and the development of curriculum, instruction, and assessment that addresses clearly identified learning goals. With a combination of theoretical grounding and practical experience, she works with educators throughout the world who are attempting to translate theory into practice. Pickering has coauthored several articles and programs, including *Dimensions of Learning Teacher's Manual* (2nd ed.) and other materials for ASCD's Dimensions of Learning series, a comprehensive model of learning that provides a framework for developing students into independent learners and complex thinkers. He recent ASCD titles include *Classroom Management That Works: Research Based Strategies for Every Teacher* (Marzano, Marzano, & Pickering, 2003); *A Handbook for Classroom Instruction That Works* (Marzano,

Paynter, Pickering, & Gaddy, 2001); and *Classroom Instruction That Works: Research-Based Strategies for Increasing Student Achievement* (Marzano, Pickering, & Pollack, 2001). She received a bachelor of science degree in English/drama education from the University of Missouri, a master's degree in school administration from the University of Denver, and a doctorate in curriculum and instruction with an emphasis on cognitive psychology from the University of Denver. Pickering can be contacted at 7009 South Curtice St., Littleton, CO 80120. Phone: 1-303-694-9899. E-mail: djplearn@hotmail.com.

# A | Templates

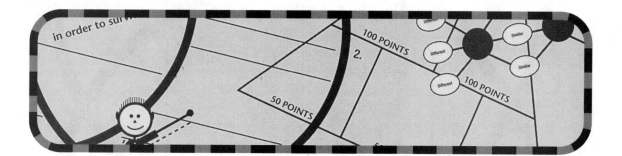

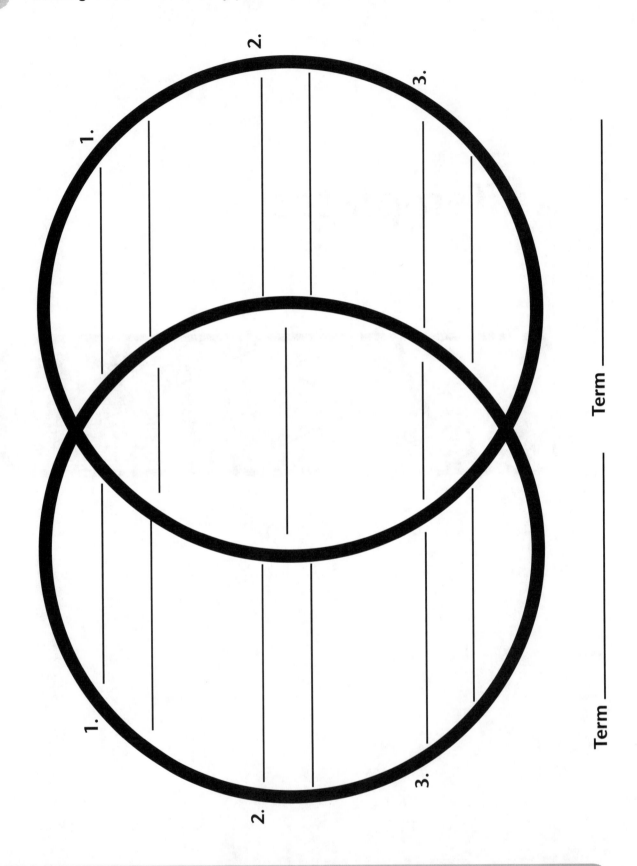

Term _____

Term _____

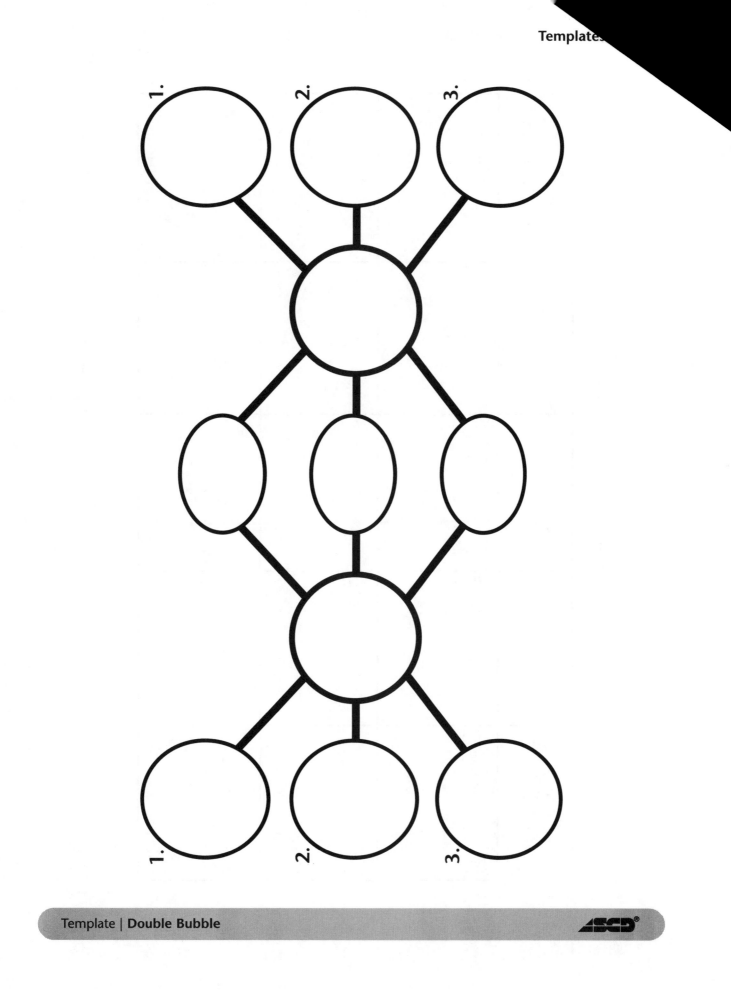

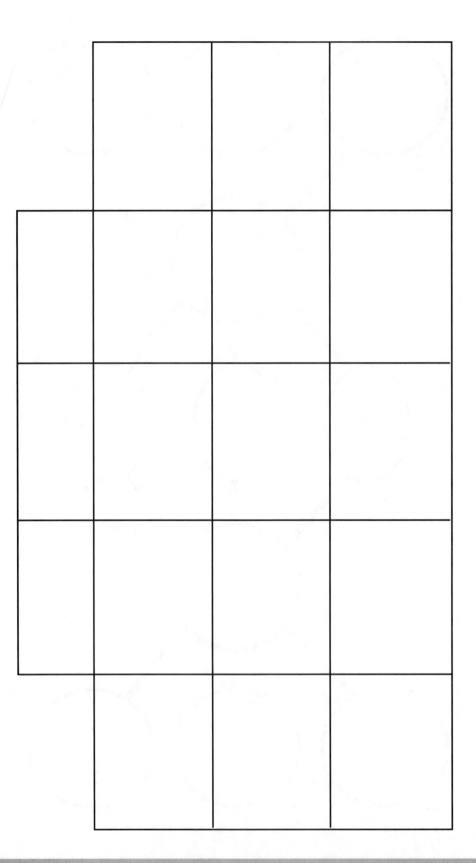

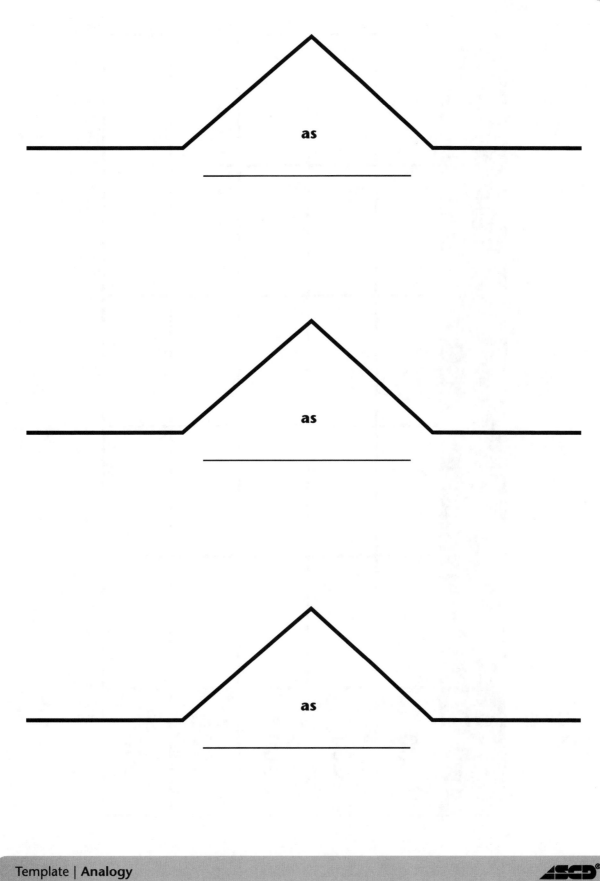

| | Science | Math | Lang. Arts | Sports/Arts | General |
|---|---|---|---|---|---|
| **100** | | | | | |
| **200** | | | | | |
| **300** | | | | | |
| **400** | | | | | |
| **500** | | | | | |

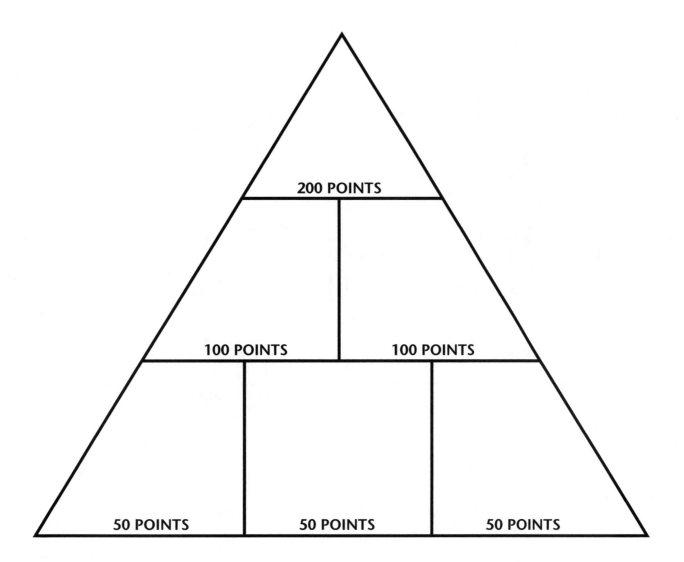

200 POINTS

100 POINTS     100 POINTS

50 POINTS     50 POINTS     50 POINTS

# B | Academic Vocabulary Word Lists

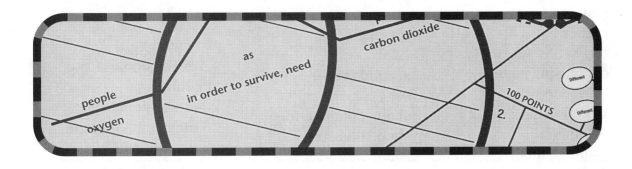

In this section, 7,923 vocabulary terms are listed for 11 subject areas:

1. Mathematics
2. Science
3. English language arts
4. History
5. Geography
6. Civics
7. Economics
8. Health
9. Physical education
10. The Arts
11. Technology

The terms for all subject areas are reported at four levels:

Level 1: grades K–2
Level 2: grades 3–5
Level 3: grades 6–8
Level 4: grades 9–12

## Vocabulary Terms

Readers should note that proper names are listed alphabetically by first name as opposed to last name. Also, some entries are alphabetized on the basis of the article *the*.

# Mathematics | Word List

## Level 1

above
addition
area
behind
below
between
calendar
cardinal number
chance
circle
clock
coin
corner
day
decreasing pattern
difference
direction
distance
estimate answer
foot (measurement)
graph
greater than
grouping
guess and check
height
hour
in front
inch
increasing pattern
inside
left
length
less than
lists
location
measuring cup
minute
model

money
near
number
number line
numeral
numeric pattern
ordinal number
orientation
outcome
outside
pattern
pattern extension
pound
prediction
rectangle
right
second (time)
set
shape combination
shape division
shape pattern
similarity
size
sound pattern
square
standard measures of
    time
standard measures of
    weight
subtraction
sum
table
temperature
temperature estimation
temperature
    measurement
time interval
triangle
under
volume

week
whole number
width
year
zero

## Level 2

2-dimensional shape
2-dimensional shape
    combination
2-dimensional shape
    decomposition
2-dimensional shape
    slide
2-dimensional shape
    turn
2-dimensional space
3-dimensional shape
3-dimensional shape
    combination
acute angle
addend
addition algorithm
angle
angle measurement tool
angle unit
area
associative property
bar graph
basic number
    combinations
capacity
centimeter
certainty (probability)
circumference
classes of triangles
cluster
common denominator

# Mathematics | Word List

### Level 2 (cont.)

common fractions
commutative property
conservation of area
constant
corresponding angles
corresponding sides
cube
cylinder
data
data cluster
data collection method
decimal
decimal addition
decimal division
decimal estimation
decimal multiplication
decimal subtraction
diagram
different size units
distributive property
dividend
divisibility
division
elapsed time
English system of
    measurement
equation
equilateral triangle
equivalent forms
equivalent fractions
equivalent
    representation
estimation
estimation of fractions
estimation of height
estimation of length
estimation of width
even numbers

event likelihood
expanded notation
extreme value
faces of a shape
factors
flip transformation
fraction
fraction addition
fraction division
fraction multiplication
fraction subtraction
fractions of different size
front-end digits
front-end estimation
function
geometric pattern
geometric patterns
    extension
gram
greatest common factor
growing pattern
histogram
horizontal axis
identity property
improbability
improper fraction
inequality
inequality solutions
intersection of shapes
invalid argument
investigation
irrelevant information in
    a problem
isosceles triangle
least common multiple
line graph
linear pattern
mass
mean
measurement

measures of central
    tendency
measures of height
measures of length
measures of width
median
meter
metric system
midpoint
mixed numbers
mode
multiple
multiplication
negative number
number of faces
number pairs
number sentence
number triplet
obtuse angle
odd numbers
open sentence
order of operations
parallel lines
parallelogram
parallelogram formula
part to whole
path
pattern addition
pattern subtraction
percent
perimeter
perpendicular lines
pie chart
positive number
prime factorization
prime number
prism
probability
process of elimination
product

### Level 2 (cont.)

proof
pyramid
quotient
rectangle formula
rectangular prism
reduced form
relative distance
relative magnitude
relative magnitude of
    fractions
relative size
relevant information in a
    problem
remainder
repeating pattern
restate a problem
reversing order of
    operations
rhombus
right angle
rotation
rounding
ruler
same size units
sample
scale
shape similarity
shape symmetry
shape transformation
shrinking pattern
sphere
standard vs.
    nonstandard units
studies
subset
subtraction algorithm
surface area
survey

symbolic representation
tallies
time zone
trial & error
triangle formula
truncation
unit conversion
unit differences
unlike denominators
valid argument
variability
Venn diagram
verbal representation of
    a problem
verification
vertical axis
volume measurement
volume of irregular
    shapes
volume of rectangular
    solids

### Level 3

3-dimensional shape
    cross section
3-dimensional space
addition of fractions
algebraic expression
algebraic expression
    expansion
algebraic representation
algebraic step function
alternate interior angle
angle bisector
approximate lines
area model
area of irregular shapes
array

axis of symmetry
base 10
base 60
benchmarking
biased sample
blueprint
box & whisker plot
certainty of conclusions
circle formula
circumference formula
combining like terms
complementary angle
complementary event
complex problem
composite number
congruence
conjecture
constant difference
constant rate of change
constant ratio
convert large number to
    small number
convert small number to
    large number
coordinate geometry
coordinate plane
coordinate system
counter example
counting procedure
cube number
cube root
cubic unit
data display error
data extreme
data gap
data set
deductive argument
deductive prediction
defining properties of
    shapes/figures

## Level 3 (cont.)

dilation
dispersion
distance formula
enlarging transformation
equal ratios
equation systems
experiment
exponent
exponential notation
fair chance
formula for missing
    values
frequency
frequency distribution
graphic representation
    of function
graphic solution
grid
growth rate
inductive reasoning
input/output table
integer
intercept
intersecting lines
irregular polygon
iterative sequence
large sample
limited sample
line symmetry
linear arithmetic
    sequence
linear equation
linear geometric
    sequence
linear units
logic ALL
logic AND
logic IF/THEN

logic NONE
logic NOT
logic OR
logic SOME
mathematical expression
maximum
method selection
minimum
multiple problem-solving
    strategies
multiple strategies for
    proofs
multiplication algorithm
mutually exclusive
    events
networks
nominal data
nondecimal numeration
    system
nonlinear equation
nonlinear function
nonroutine vs. routine
    problems
number property
number systems
number theory
odds
ordered pairs
outliers
overestimation
parallel figures
pattern division
pattern multiplication
pattern recognition
percents above 100
percents below 1
perimeter formula
perpendicular bisector
perspective
pictorial representation

place holder
planar cross section
plane
plane figure
polygon
precision of
    measurement
prime factor
problem formulation
problem space
problem types
projection
proportion
proportional gain
quadratic equation
quadrilateral
random number
random sample
random variable
range
range of estimations
rate
rate of change
rational number
rectangular coordinates
recursive sequence
reference set
reflection
    transformation
relative frequency
relatively prime
reliability
Roman numeral
root
rotation symmetry
sample selection
    techniques
sample space
sampling error
scale drawing

# Mathematics | Word List

### Level 3 (cont.)

scale map
scale transformation
scatter plot
scientific notation
sequence
shrinking transformation
significant digits
similar proportions
similarity vs. congruence
simplification
slide transformation
slope
slope intercept formula
solid figure
solution algorithm
solution probabilities
spreadsheet
square number
square root
square units
stem & leaf plot
straight edge & compass
substitution for
    unknowns
supplementary angle
table representation of
    functions
table representation of
    probability
tessellation
tetrahedron
theoretical probability
thermometer
trapezoid formula
tree diagram model
triangle sides
underestimation
unit size

unknown
variable
variable change
vertex
volume formula
volume of cylinder
volume of prism
volume of pyramid
work backward
written representation

### Level 4

absolute error
absolute function
absolute value
acceleration
add radical expressions
addition counting
    procedure
algebraic function
angle of depression
arc
area under curve
asymptote of function
base e
binary system
bivariate data
bivariate data
    transformation
bivariate distribution
Cartesian coordinates
categorical data
central angle
central limit theorem
chord
circle without center
circular function
classes of functions

combination
complex number
compound event
compound interest
conditional probability
confidence interval
conjugate complex
    number
continuity
continuous probability
    distribution
control group
correlation
cosine
critical paths method
curve fitting
curve fitting median
    method
decibel
density
dependent events
derivation
dilation of object in a
    plane
direct function
direct measure
discrete probability
discrete probability
    distribution
divide radical
    expressions
domain of function
empirical verification
equivalent forms of
    equations
equivalent forms of
    inequalities
expected value
experimental design
experimental probability

## Level 4 (cont.)

exponent
exponential function
factorial
factorial notation
Fibonacci sequence
finite graph
force
formal mathematical
  induction
fraction inversion
function composition
function notation
geometric function
global/local behavior
imaginary number
independent events
independent trials
indirect measure
inflection
interest
inverse function
irrational number
isometry
law of large numbers
law of probability
limit
line equation
line segment
line segment congruence
line segment similarity
line through point not on
  a line
linear
log function
logarithm
logarithmic function
mathematical theories
matrix

matrix addition
matrix division
matrix equation
matrix inversion
matrix multiplication
matrix subtraction
minimum/maximum of
  function
monitor progress of a
  problem
monomial
Monte Carlo simulation
multiply radical
  expressions
natural log
natural number
nature of deduction
negative exponent
normal curve
number subsystems
parallel box plot
parameter
parameter estimate
parametric equation
periodic function
permutation
phase shift
pi
point of tangency
polar coordinates
polynomial
polynomial addition
polynomial division
polynomial function
polynomial
  multiplication
polynomial solution by
  bisection
polynomial solution by
  sign change

polynomial solution
  successive approxi-
  mation
polynomial subtraction
population
postulate
powers
precision of estimation
probability distribution
proof paragraph
protractor
Pythagorean theorem
quartile deviation
radical expression
radical function
radius
random sampling
  technique
range of function
rational function
real numbers
real-world function
reciprocal
recurrence equation
recurrence relationship
recursive equation
reflection in plane
reflection in space
regression coefficient
regression line
relative error
representativeness of
  sample
Richter scale
right triangle geometry
roots & real numbers
roots to determine cost
roots to determine profit
roots to determine
  revenue

### Level 4 (cont.)

rotation in plane
sample statistic
sampling distribution
scalar
series
series circuit
sigma notation
similar figures
sine
sinusoidal function
smallest set of rules
speed
spurious correlation
standard deviation
statistical experiment
statistical regression
statistic
step function

strategy efficiency
strategy generation
    technique
subtract radical
    expressions
successive
    approximations
summary statistic
surface area cone
surface area cylinder
surface area sphere
synthetic geometry
systems of inequalities
tangent
term
theorem
theorem direct proof
theorem indirect proof
transversal
treatment group

trigonometric ratio
trigonometric relation
truth table proof
two-way tables
U.S. customary system
unit analysis
univariate data
univariate distribution
upper/lower bounds
validity
variance
vector
vector addition
vector division
vector multiplication
vector subtraction
velocity
vertex edge graph

# Science | Word List

## Level 1

air
animal features
balance
behavior pattern
boulder
burning
chart
circular motion
cloud
color
computer
daily weather pattern
day
death
dinosaur
dissolving
distance
diversity of life
Earth materials
Earth's gravity
Earth's rotation
egg
energy
food
freezing
gas
growth
habitat
heat
horsetail tree
individual differences
insect
light
liquid
liquid water
location
machine
magnet

magnification
magnifier
mammoth
mixture
month
Moon
motion
night
observation
ocean
parent
parent/offspring
    similarity
pebble
plant
plant growth
position
precipitation
prediction
prehistoric animals
properties of light
pulling
pushing
reasoning
requirements for life
rock characteristics
ruler
salt water
sand
science
scientist
seasonal change
seasonal weather pattern
shape
shelter
similarities & differences
    among organisms
size
sky
soil

solid rock
sound
star
star age
star brightness
states of matter
straight-line motion
Sun's position
Sun's size
teamwork
temperature
the senses
thermometer
universe
vibration
water
weather
weather conditions
weather patterns
week
weight
wind
year
zigzag motion

## Level 2

ability to support life
acceleration
air movement
animal product
apparent movement of
    the planets
apparent movement of
    the stars
apparent movement of
    the Sun
applied force
astronomical distance

## Level 2 (cont.)

astronomical object
astronomical size
astronomy
battery
bedrock
beneficial change
birth
body of water
boiling point
bones/no bones
calculator
cause & effect
change of direction
change of motion
change of speed
changes in the Earth's
   surface
characteristics of air
charge attraction
charge repulsion
classification of
   substances
competition
composition of matter
condensation
conduction
conductivity
conductor
conservation of mass
conservation of matter
constellation
control of variables
controlled experiment
cooling
core
data analysis
data interpretation
data presentation

density
detrimental change
disease
drought
Earth's axis
Earth's orbit
Earth's surface
Earth's temperature
earthquake
electrical charge
electrical circuit
electrical current
electricity
energy transfer
engineering
environment
environmental changes
environmental
   conditions
erosion
evaporation
external cue
extinction
food chain
food web
force strength
forms of energy
forms of water
formula
fossil
fossil evidence
fresh water
friction
gases of the atmosphere
generator
glacial movement
glacier
graduated cylinder
graph
ground water

heat conduction
heat transfer
herbivore
history of science
inherited characteristic
land form
landslide
life cycle
light absorption
light emission
light reflection
light refraction
living organism
logical argument
magnetic attraction
magnetic repulsion
mass
measurement of motion
melting point
metal
microscope
migration
mineral
Moon's orbit
Moon's phases
naturalistic observation
nutrients
ocean currents *removed*
offspring
oil
omnivore
ongoing process of
   science
organism
outer space
phase change
photosynthetic plants
physical properties
physical setting
pitch

# Science | Word List

### Level 2 (cont.)

planet
plant organ
plant product
plant root
plant/animal
pollution
population
population density
position over time
predator
prehistoric environment
prehistoric organisms
properties of soil
properties of sound
properties of water
question formulation
recycle *removed*
relative position
replicable experiment
reproducible result
reproduction
resource availability
rock breakage
rock composition
rock cycle
scientific equipment
scientific evidence
scientific experiment
soil color
soil composition
soil texture
solar system
solubility
stored energy
survival of organisms
technology
telescope
tide

volcanic eruption
water capacity
weathered rock
weathering
wind patterns

### Level 3

acquired trait
adaptive characteristics
air mass circulation
alternative explanation
    of data
animal nervous systems
asexual reproduction
asteroid
asteroid impact
asteroid movement
    patterns
atmosphere
atmospheric
    composition
atmospheric layers
atmospheric pressure
atom
atomic arrangement
balanced force
behavioral change in
    organisms
behavioral response to
    stimuli
bias
body plan
carrying capacity
celestial body
cell
cell division
cell growth
characteristics of life

chemical change
chemical compound
chemical element
chemical energy
chemical properties of
    substances
chemical reaction
circulatory system
classification of
    organisms
climate
climate change
climatic pattern
closed system
color of light
comet
comet impact
comet movement
    patterns
common ancestry
concentration of
    reactants
confirmation by
    observation
conflicting
    interpretations
conservation of energy
constant speed
continuation of species
crustal deformation
crustal plate movement
crystal
debris
deceleration
decomposer
digestive system
direction of a force
direction of motion
displacement of results
Earth system

# Science | Word List

## Level 3 (cont.)

Earth's age
Earth's atmosphere
Earth's climate
Earth's crust
Earth's layers
eclipse
ecological role
ecosystem
egg cell
electric current
electrical energy
element stability
emergence of life forms
energy source
erosion resistance
ethics in science
evaluation of science
    process
evidence from
    sedimentary rock
excretory system
experimental
    confirmation
experimental control
external feature
faulty reasoning
filtering
food oxidization
forms of matter
fossil record
fundamental unit of life
fungus
galaxy
Galileo
gene
geologic evidence
geologic force
geological shift

gravitational force
Greek basic four
    elements
habits of mind
heat convection
heat emission
heat energy
heat radiation
heat retention
hereditary information
homeostasis
host
hydrosphere
hypothesis
hypothesis testing
igneous rock
immune system
inertia
infection
informed subject
infrared radiation
insulator
intellectual honesty
interdependence of
    organisms
internal cue
internal structure
invertebrate
kinetic energy
lever arm
life form change
life-sustaining functions
light scattering
light transmission
light wavelength
light year
lithosphere
logic
Louis Pasteur
mantle

Marie Curie
mathematical model
mechanical energy
mechanical motion
metal reactivity
metamorphic rock
meteor
meteor impact
meteor movement
    patterns
Milky Way galaxy
molecular arrangement
molecular motion
molecule
multicellular organism
muscular system
mutualism
nervous system
Newton's Laws of
    Motion
nonmetal reactivity
nonreactive gas
nuclear reaction
organ
organ system
organism system failure
oxidation
oxygen
parasite
particle ring
peer review
percolation
photosynthesis
physiological change
Pierre Curie
planet composition
planet orbits
planet size
planet surface features
plant tissue

# Science | Word List

### Level 3 (cont.)

polygenic trait
predation
prey
properties of elements
pulley
radiation
reaction rate
recrystallization
recycling of matter
reproductive system
research question
respiration
respiratory system
right of refusal
risk & benefit
rock layer movement
rusting
satellite
scientific interpretation
scientific method
scientific skepticism
screening
sediment deposition
sedimentary rock
sedimentation
separation method
sexual reproduction
skeletal system
soil erosion
soil fertility
solar system formation
specialized cell
specialized organ
specialized tissue
species
species diversity
speed
sperm

sperm cell
sunlight reflection
surface area of reactants
surface run-off
taxonomy
theoretical model
tissue
tolerance of ambiguity
unbalanced force
unicellular organism
unity of life
universal solvent
vertebrate
visible light
water cycle
wavelength

### Level 4

abiotic components of
    ecosystems
accelerator
acid/base reactions
actual mass
advection
age of the universe
Albert Einstein
Alfred Wegener
amino acid sequence
anatomical
    characteristic
Antoine Lavoisier
atmospheric change
atomic bomb
atomic bonding
    principles
atomic configuration
atomic energy
atomic mass

atomic motion
atomic nucleus
atomic number
atomic reaction
atomic theory
atomic weight
Avogadro's hypothesis
Bernoulli's principle
Big Bang theory
biochemical
    characteristic
biological adaptation
biological evolution
biological molecule
breakdown of food
    molecules
buoyancy
carbon
carbon atom
carbon cycle
carbon dioxide
catalyst
cell function
cell membrane
cell nucleus
cell organelle
cell wall
cellular communication
cellular differentiation
cellular energy
    conversion
cellular regulation
cellular response
cellular waste disposal
charged object
Charles Darwin
Charles Lyell
chemical bond
chemical organization of
    organisms

# Science | Word List

## Level 4 (cont.)

chemical properties of
elements
chemical reaction rate
chloroplast
chromatography
chromosome
chromosome pair
composition of the
universe
convection
convection current
Copernican revolution
Copernicus
Coulomb's law
criteria for acceptance
crystalline solid
cytoplasm
data reduction
decay rate
degree of kinship
derived characteristic
disclosure of methods &
procedures
DNA
DNA molecule
DNA replication
DNA sequence
DNA structure
DNA subunit
dominant trait
Doppler effect
drag
Earth's elements
Earth's external energy
sources
Earth's formation
Earth's internal energy
sources

elasticity
electric force
electric motor
electric potential
electrically neutral
electromagnetic field
electromagnetic force
electromagnetic
radiation
electromagnetic
spectrum
electromagnetic wave
electron
electron configuration
electron sharing
electron transfer
elementary particle
elements of matter
elimination of matter &
energy
elliptical orbits
embryo formation
empirical standards
endothermic reaction
energy requirements of
living systems
Enrico Fermi
entropy
enzyme
equal & opposite force
equilibrium of
ecosystems
Ernest Rutherford
evidence for the Big
Bang theory
evidence for the expan-
sion of the universe
evidence for the unity
among organisms
excitatory molecule

exothermic reaction
experimental method
F=ma
Fahrenheit
filial generation
flow of energy
flow of matter
fluid resistance
foot pound
formation of polymers
fossil fuels
gamma ray
gene encoding
gene expression
general theory of
relativity
genetic diversity
genetic mutation
genetic variation
geochemical cycle
geologic time
geologic time scale
geological dating
Gregor Mendel
germ theory
Golgi apparatus
gravitational energy
greenhouse gas
Halley's comet
harvesting of resources
history of the universe
human genetics
human modification of
ecosystems
hydrogen bomb
hydrogen ion
inertial frame of
reference
inhibitory molecule
inverse square law

# Science | Word List

## Level 4 (cont.)

ion
ionic motion
isotope
Johannes Kepler
John Dalton
Kelvin (temperature)
Lise Meitner
mass to energy
    conversion
meiosis
Mendelian genetics
metallic surface
method of investigation
microwave
mitochondrion
mitosis
molar volume
mole
molecular energy
molecular synthesis
molten rock
mountain building
moving electrical charge
moving magnet
natural selection
net force
neuron
neurotransmitter
neutron
new gene combinations
Newtonian mechanics
nitrogen
nitrogen cycle
nuclear fission
nuclear force
nuclear fusion
nuclear mass
nuclear stability

nucleated cell
ocean layers
ohm
organic compound
    synthesis
organic matter
origin of life
origin of the universe
oxidation-reduction
    reactions
ozone
paradigm shift
parental generation
particle emission
periodic table of the
    elements
photosynthesizing
    organism
phylogenetics
plate boundary
plate collision
plate tectonics
potential energy
pressure
properties of reactants
properties of waves
protein
protein structure
protein synthesis
proton
Ptolemy
quantum of energy
radical reaction
radio wave
radioactive dating
radioactive decay
radioactive isotope
rate of nuclear decay
recessive trait

recombination of
    chemical elements
recombination of genetic
    material
relative mass
relative motion
release of energy
reproductive capacity
reproductive value of
    traits
revision of scientific
    theories
rock sequence
rules of evidence
sea floor spreading
segregation
seismic wave
selective gene
    expression
semiconductor
sex cell
sex chromosomes
sex-linked trait
shared characteristic
sound wave
space probe
special theory of
    relativity
speciation
speed of light
spontaneous nuclear
    reaction
star composition
star destruction
star formation
star size
star system
star temperature
star types
stellar energy

### Level 4 (cont.)

storage of genetic
   information
Sun's radiation
superconductor
survival value of traits
synthetic polymer
thermal equilibrium
torque

transforming matter
   and/or energy
transport of cell materials
transporting matter
   and/or energy
ultraviolet radiation
unequal heating of air
unequal heating of land
   masses
unequal heating of oceans

vacuole
viscosity
water wave
wave amplitude
wave packet
wave source
weight of subatomic
   particles
x-ray

# English Language Arts | Word List

## Level 1

alphabet
author
back cover
beginning consonant
blend
book
cartoon
chapter
character
composition
comprehension
consonant blend
conversation
cover
date
dictionary
discussion
drawing
ending consonant
everyday language
fairy tale
first name
folktale
follow/give directions
front cover
group discussion
guest speaker
keyboarding
language
last name
letter
letter-sound relationship
listening skill
long vowel
lowercase
magazine
main character
main idea

map
margin
mental image
message
movie
newspaper
number word
order of events
parts of a book
photographer
picture book
picture dictionary
poem
predictable book
prewriting
print
publish
purpose
question
reread
respond to literature
retell
rhyme
sentence
short vowel
sight word
sign
speech
spelling
spelling pattern
symbol
table of contents
take turns
television program
textbook
theater
title
title page
typing
uppercase

videotape
villain
vocabulary
vowel combination
vowel sound

## Level 2

abbreviation
action verb
action word
actor
adjective
adverb
advertisement
affix
animation
antonym
apology
apostrophe
appendix
asking permission
audience
audiotape
auxiliary verb
brainstorm
capitalization
card catalog
cause and effect
central idea
chapter title
character development
chart
checklist
children's literature
chronological order
citation
closing sentence
colon

## Level 2 (cont.)

comma
command
commercial
common noun
compare & contrast
complete sentence
complex sentence
compound word
concluding statement
conclusion
consonant substitution
construct meaning
content-area vocabulary
context clue
contraction
contrast
cue
cursive
custom
declarative sentence
decode
definition
detail
diary
direct quote
directions
director
discussion leader
double negative
draft
drama
e-mail
edit
encyclopedia
ending
essay
example
explanation

expression
fable
facial expression
fantasy
fiction
first person
form
friendly letter
genre
gesture
glossary
grammar
graphic artist
graphic organizer
graphics
greeting
guide words
heading
headline
host
hostess
how question
humor
illustration
imagery
indentation
index
inference
Internet
interrogative sentence
introduction
investigate
invitation
irregular plural noun
journal
key word
learning log
legend
letter of request
linking verb

list
listening comprehension
literature
meaning clue
memory aid
minor character
miscue
mood
motive
multimeaning word
multiple drafts
multiple sources
mystery
myth
negative
news
newspaper section
nonfiction
notes
noun
novel
numerical adjective
object
opinion
oral presentation
oral report
organization
outline
pamphlet
paragraph
passage
past tense
peer review
pen pal
period
personal letter
personal pronoun
phone directory
phonetic analysis
phrase

### Level 2 (cont.)

pitch
plot
plot development
point of view
posing a question
possessive noun
possessive pronoun
posture
preface
prefix
preposition
prepositional phrase
presentation
preview
prior knowledge
pronoun
pronunciation
proofread
prop
proper noun
punctuation
question mark
quotation
quotation marks
r-controlled
radio program
rating
reading strategy
reading vocabulary
regular plural noun
regular verb
request
revise
rhyming dictionary
role playing
root word
rules of conversation
scan

science fiction
second person
sensory image
sentence structure
sequential order
setting
short story
signature
singular noun
skim
sound effect
source
special effect
spoken text
stay on topic
story element
story map
story structure
subject
subject-verb agreement
suffix
summarize
summary
summary sentence
supporting detail
suspense
syllabication
syllable
symbolism
synonym
table
tall tale
target language
tense
text
thank you letter
theme
theme music
thesaurus
third person

time line
tone
topic sentence
typeface
usage
verb
voice
voice level
volume
Web site
when question
where question
why question
word choice
word family
word search
written directions
written exchange

### Level 3

action segment
active listener
adjective clause
adjective phrase
adverb clause
adverb phrase
almanac
Anglo-Saxon affix
Anglo-Saxon root
argumentation
atlas
author's purpose
autobiography
background knowledge
bibliography
biographical sketch
biography
body language

## Level 3 (cont.)

body of the text
broadcast
broadcast advertising
business letter
camera angle
camera shot
caption
catalog
CD-ROM
character trait
children's program
chronology
clarification
climax
close-up
closing
clue
common feature
comparative adjective
compile
composition structure
compound sentence
compound verb
conjunction
contract
convention
coordinating
   conjunction
criticism
cross-reference
current affairs
demonstrative pronoun
derivation
description
descriptive language
diagram
dialect
dialogue

document
documentary
editorial
elaboration
electronic media
enunciation
episode
etiquette
etymology
exclamation mark
exclamatory sentence
explicit/implicit
exposition
extend invitation
extraneous information
eye contact
facilitator
fact vs. opinion
familiar idiom
familiar interaction
feature story
feedback
figurative language
figure of speech
film director
flashback
follow-up sentence
footnote
foreign word
foreshadowing
formal language
formal speech
format
fully developed
   character
gender
generalization
glittering generality
grammatical form
Greek affix

Greek root
high-frequency word
historical fiction
historical theme
homonym
homophone
hyphen
imperative sentence
inconsistency
independent clause
informal language
information source
interjection
interpretation
interview
intonation
irregular verb
italics
jargon
juxtaposition
knowledge base
language convention
layout
lecture
line (in a play)
literal phrase
log
logic
logical argument
logo
manner of speech
mass media
mechanics (language)
media type
metaphor
meter
modifier
multimedia presentation
musical
narration

## Level 3 (cont.)

native culture
native speaker
news broadcast
news bulletin
nonverbal cue
object pronoun
objective view
oral tradition
pacing
page format
parallel episodes
parallel structure
paraphrase
peer-response group
periodical
personal narrative
personification
perspective
persuasion
phrase grouping
physical description
physical gesture
plagiarism
poetic element
polite form
political cartoonist
political speech
positive adjective
predicate adjective
present tense
private audience
problem-solution
producer
programming
projection
pronominal adjective
proper adjective
proverb

public audience
public opinion trend
publication date
pull-down menu
quiz show
*Reader's Guide to
    Periodical Literature*
recitation
recurring theme
reference source
relative pronoun
relevant detail
rephrasing
report
representation
research paper
resolution
resource material
restatement
rhythm
sales technique
salutation
saying
scriptwriter
self-correction
sentence combining
shades of meaning
simile
simple sentence
sitcom
skit
slang
slanted material
small talk
software
sound system
special interests
specialized language
speech pattern
speed reading

stereotype
stress
stylistic feature
subject pronoun
subjective view
subliminal message
subordinate character
subordinating
    conjunction
subplot
superlative adjective
supernatural tale
syllabic system
syntax
synthesize
tabloid newspaper
talk show
target audience
technical directions
technical language
tempo
tension (in a story)
textual clue
time lapse
transition
translate
trickster tale
verb phrase
verbal cue
vernacular dialect
viewer perception
viewpoint
visual aid
voice inflection
word borrowing
word origin
word play

## Level 4

acronym
advertising code
advertising copy
aesthetic purpose
aesthetic quality
allegory
alliteration
allusion
ambience
ambiguity
American literature
American Psychological
   Association
analogy
ancient literature
anecdotal scripting
anecdote
annotated bibliography
appeal to authority
appeal to emotion
appeal to logic
archetype
articulation
artifact
assonance
attack ad hominem
author's bias
autobiographical
   narrative
ballad
bandwagon
belief system
bias
Bible
biographical narrative
blurring of genres
bolding
British literature

bylaw
celebrity endorsement
censorship
characterization
cinematographer
circumlocution
clarity of purpose
clincher sentence
cognate
coherence
cohesion
collective noun
commercialization
compound adjective
compound noun
compound personal
   pronoun
compound-complex
   sentence
computer-generated
   image
concept
conceptual map
conjunctive adverb
connotative meaning
consonance
consumer document
context
contrasting expressions
controlling idea
copyright law
correlative conjunction
counter argument
couplet
credibility
credit
criteria
critical standard
cultural agency
cultural expression

cultural influence
cultural nuance
cultural theme
cutline
dash
debate
deconstruct
delivery
denotative meaning
dictation
diction
digressive time
direct address
directionality
divided quotation
drama-documentary
dramatic dialogue
dramatic mood change
emotional appeal
emphasis
epic
ethics
exaggerated claim
excerpt
expressive writing
extended quotation
external/internal conflict
false causality
faulty mode of persuasion
FCC regulation
feature article
fictional narrative
field study
film review
filter (in photography)
friendly audience
future perfect verb tense
hierarchic structure
Homeric Greek literature
hostile audience

## Level 4 (cont.)

hyperbole
idiom
incongruity
indefinite adjective
indefinite pronoun
inflection
interior monologue
internal conflict
interrogative pronoun
irony
job application
job interview
Latin affix
Latin root
leave-taking
limited point of view
literary criticism
literary device
literature review
logical fallacy
logographic system
lyric poem
marketing
media-generated image
medieval literature
medium
memorandum
methodology
microfiche
Modern Language
    Association
modern literature
modulation
mythology
narrator
negotiate
neoclassic literature
norm

noun clause
noun phrase
nuance
ode
omniscient point of view
onomatopoeia
opening monologue
overgeneralization
overstatement
overview
packaging
parable
parody
past perfect verb tense
pastoral
performance review
persona
personal space
philosophical
    assumption
poise
policy statement
present perfect verb
    tense
primary source
production cost
progressive verb form
propaganda
proposition of fact
    speech
proposition of policy
    speech
proposition of problem
    speech
proposition of value
    speech
questionnaire
reaction shot
readability
red herring

redraft
reflexive pronoun
repeats
resume
rhetorical device
rhetorical question
romantic period literature
sarcasm
satire
secondary source
semicolon
set design
soap opera
sociocultural context
soliloquy
somber lighting
speech action
speed writing
standard English
status indicator
stream of consciousness
structural analysis
style sheet format
subvocalize
telephone information
    service
temporal change
text boundary
text feature
text structure
thesis
thesis statement
transparency
truth in advertising
understatement
universal theme
visual text
warranty
word processing
word reference

## Level 1

Abraham Lincoln
America
American Revolution, 1776
ancient time
archeological evidence
argument
automobile
beginning
behavior
belief
Benjamin Franklin
bow and arrow
bridge
building
calendar time
camel caravan
cause
celebration
ceremony
chariot
Christmas
Christopher Columbus
city
colonial community
common good
community
country
cowboy
crop
cultural tradition
daily life
dance
day
decade
democracy
disagreement
domesticated animal

education
ending date
England
English colony
environment
equality
event
expansion
explorer
fable
family history
family life
farm
father of our country
folktale
Fourth of July
freedom
future
generation
geography
George Washington
goods
government
group membership
harvest festival
heroism
history
holiday
houses of worship
housing
human rights
hunger
hunter/gatherer
idea
independence
individual rights
invention
job
journey
law

leader
legend
liberty
Liberty Bell
lifestyle
local history
Martin Luther King Jr.
Martin Luther King Jr. Day
Memorial Day
middle
money
month
monument
myth
nation
national flag
national holiday
Native American
newcomer
nonmotorized vehicle
oral tradition
origin
past
photograph
picture time line
pioneer
place-name
plant cultivation
Pledge of Allegiance
Plymouth
pony express
prairie
present
printing press
radio
recent past
recreation
region
regional folk hero

### Level 1 (cont.)

regional song
religion
resistance
respect for others
responsibility
revolution
role
rules
satellite system
sculpture
senior citizen home
services
society
soup kitchen
state
steam engine
steamship
surplus food
symbol
tall tale
team member
technology
telegraph
temple
territory
Thanksgiving
Thomas Jefferson
time line
today
tomorrow
tool
town
trade
trail
transportation
travel
United States
vote

war
week
wheel
White House
worker
world
year
yesterday

### Level 2

A.D.
abolition movement
abolitionist
acceptable behavior
Adolf Hitler
Africa
African American
African slave trade
agriculture
aircraft carrier
Alaska
Alexander Graham Bell
alliance
Allied Powers
Amelia Earhart
American Indian chief
American society
American symbol
Americas, the
ancestor worship
ancient Greece
ancient Rome
Angel Island
annexation
Anno Domini
anti-Chinese movement
aqueduct
archeologist
archeology

architect
architecture
armed forces
artifact
artistic expression
Asia
Asian American
Asian Pacific settler
assembly line
Astoria
astrolabe
attitudes
author's interpretation
autobiography
aviation
Aztec
ballad
Bantu migrations in
    Africa
B.C., Before Christ
B.C.E., Before the
    Common Era
behavior consequence
behavior pattern
Bering land bridge
Betty Zane
big business
Bill of Rights
Billy the Kid
biography
Black Hawk War
blue-collar worker
Booker T. Washington
Boston Tea Party
Braille alphabet
Brer Rabbit
Britain
British Isle
bronze tool-making
    technology

# General History | Word List

**Level 2 (cont.)**

California
camel
campaign
Canada
canal system
Caribbean
caste system
castle
cattle herders
C.E.
Central Africa
Central America
century
Cesar Chavez
character trait
Cherokee
Cherokee Trail of Tears
China
Chinese community
Chinese New Year
Christian
Christianity
chronology
Cinco de Mayo
citizenship
civil liberties
civil rights
civil rights movement
civil war
Civil War (U.S.)
Clara Barton
class
climate changes
coal mining
coffee trade
Cold War
colonial government
colonial period

colonist
colony
Columbian Exchange
Columbus
commercial advertising
commercial center
Common Era
common man
communication
    technology
communism
compass
computer technology
conquest
constitution
convent
corruption
country of origin
court
craft
credibility
Cuba
Cuban Missile Crisis
cultural contact
cuneiform
custom
Daniel Boone
Davey Crockett
debt
Declaration of
    Independence
delegated power
democratic values
developing country
development
diplomacy
direct experience
discovery
disease
document

dugout Phoenician ship
Dust Bowl
Dutch
early Middle Ages
earnings
earthquake
East Asia
Eastern Europe
Eastern Hemisphere
economic
    interdependence
economic system
Egypt
Egyptian time
Eleanor Roosevelt
elected representative
electricity
Elizabeth Blackwell
Ellis Island
emancipation
Emancipation
    Proclamation
emperor
empire
employment
Enlightenment
entertainment industry
equal rights
era
Eric the Red
Erie Canal
ethnic diversity
ethnic tradition
Europe
European colonization
European Crusades
European explorer
European settler
expedition
extended family

## Level 2 (cont.)

eyewitness account
factory
family alliance
family farm
family role
famine
Far West
farming methods
Ferdinand Magellan
fertilizer
first inhabitant
fishing community
flooding pattern
food production
food storage
forced relocation
foreign policy
foreign trade
former master
former slave
France
Francisco Franco
Franklin D. Roosevelt
Frederick Douglass
freedom of expression
freedom of religion
freedom of speech
French colony
French Revolution
frontier
frontiersman
Galileo
geographic border
geology
George Bush
George W. Bush
George Washington
    Carver

Gerald Ford
Germany
Geronimo
gold production
Great Depression
group behavior
group expectations
gunpowder
Hanging Gardens of
    Babylon
Harriet Tubman
Hawaii
Hawaiian culture
hemisphere
Henry Ford
hieroglyphic
historian
historic figure
historical document
historical map
home country
home front
homeless
Hopi
household appliance
human cost
hymn
immigrant
immigration
Incan Empire
Incan highway
independence movement
Indian time
indigenous people
industrial development
Industrial Revolution
industrial society
infectious disease
institution
interest group

international conflict
Internet, the
interpretation
interstate highway
    system
Inuit
iron
iron tools and weapons
Iroquois
Islam
Islamic law
Israel
Italy
Jackie Robinson
Jacques Cartier
James Armistead
Japan
Jedediah Smith
Jesus of Nazareth
Jew
Jewish time
Joe Magarac
John Glenn
John Henry
Jonas Salk
Judaism
justice
kingdom
labor
Labor Day
labor movement
land use
landowner
landscape
Latin America
law and order
League of Nations
Lee Iaccoca
leisure activity
lesson of history

## Level 2 (cont.)

life experience
Lincoln Memorial
literacy
literacy rate
local resource
London
long-distance trade
Louis Pasteur
low-income area
lunar year
luxury goods
Lydia Darragh
majority rule
Mali
manor
manufacturing
Marco Polo
Marie Curie
mass advertising
mass media
mass production
Mayan calendar
Mayflower Compact
media
medical advance
Medieval Europe
merchant
Mexican-American war
Mexican migrant worker
Mexico
middle class
Middle East
middle passage
migrant
migration
military power
mill
mining town

minority rights
missionary
mode of communication
modern democratic
    thought
modernization
monk
Monroe Doctrine
Moslem
mother country
motive
motorized vehicle
motto
mountain man
mummification
Muslim
Muslim time
Nathan Beman
national park
national symbol
Native American
    ancestors
Native American land
    holdings
Native American tribe
natural environment
natural resource
naval warfare
navigation
New England
New England colonies
New England mill town
New Orleans
New York
newspaper account
Nez Perce
nonviolent resistance
norm
Norse long ship
North America

nuclear technology
occupation
ocean currents
official
Old Northwest
outlaw
overland trade route
overseas trade
Pacific, the
Pacific Rim economy
Pacific Theater
Palestine
parables
Paris
patriot
pattern of change
Paul Bunyan
peacekeeper
peasant
Pecos Bill
period of history
personal values
Philadelphia
physical geography
pictograph
pilgrim
plague
planned city
plantation
plantation colony
point of view
policy issue
political cartoon
political geography
pollution
popular culture
popular figure
popular uprising
population
population growth

## Level 2 (cont.)

postwar period
pottery
poverty
power by the people
Presidents Day
principles
primary source
private life
production
professional sport
property ownership
protest
proverb
Pueblo
Puerto Rico
Puritan values
pyramids
race relations
racial group
rail transportation
railroad construction
ranching
rapid transit
reconstruction
reform
reformer
religious freedom
religious revival
reservation
revolutionary
  government
right to hold office
right to life, liberty, and
  the pursuit of
  happiness
right to vote
right to work
ritual

road system
rocketry
Roman Empire
Roman Republic
Roman system of roads
Rome
Rosa Parks
ruling class
rural area
Russia
Russian peasantry
Sacramento
Sally Ride
San Antonio
San Francisco
Scandinavia
school attendance
scientific breakthrough
secondary source
separation of church and
  state
separation of powers
settlement
settler
Seven Years' War
ship design
silver production
Sioux
Sitka
slave
slave holder
slave rebellion
slave trade
slogan
smuggling
social class
social reform
solar system
solar year
Sojourner Truth

Southeast Asia
Southwest
Southwest Asia
Soviet Union
space exploration
Spain
Spanish-American War
Spanish colony
spectator sport
square rigger
St. Augustine
statehood
Statue of Liberty
steam locomotive
steel construction
street gang
submarine
suburb
sugar cane
superstition
Susan B. Anthony
systems of roads
tactic
tax
Tecumseh
Ten Commandments
tenant
Tenochtitlán
textile industry
Timbuktu
tobacco
tolerance
trade route
tradition
transport system
transportation hub
tribute
turning point in human
  history
twentieth century

## Level 2 (cont.)

unification
United Nations
United States
   Constitution
university
urban center
urban community
vaccine
Vasco da Gama
Versailles
Versailles Treaty
Veterans Day
veterans' memorial
Vietnam
Vietnam War
Vietnamese boat people
Vincennes
volunteer
voting rights
W. E. B. DuBois
weaving
Western Europe
Western Hemisphere
white-collar worker
Williamsburg
women's movement
Woodrow Wilson
working conditions
workplace
world economy
world population growth
World War I
World War II
written code
written language
written record
Zheng He

## Level 3

adaptation
agrarian society
agribusiness
agricultural economy
agricultural lifestyle
agricultural technology
anthropologist
antibiotics
armed revolution
astronomical discovery
astronomy
atomic bomb
authoritarian rule
Batu
Benin
Bill Clinton
birth rate
black majority
blind respect
boundary dispute
bourgeoisie
British rule
bronze casting
brush painting
business practice
capitalism
capitalist economy
Catholic Christianity
Catholic Church
chance event
charter document
chattel slavery
checks and balances
child labor
Chinese Revolution
Christian beliefs
civil disobedience
civil service examination

civil service reform
civilian
civilian population
civilization
clergy
coerced labor
cohesion
collectivization
colonization
colony in Massachusetts
commercialization
communal life
communist country
Communist Party
conflict resolution
conservation movement
conservatism
contemporary
   democracy
convert
cosmos
court packing
crop rotation
cross-cultural contact
cultural exchange
cultural heritage
cultural integration
daily survival skill
dating methods
death rate
debtor class
demographic shift
depression
desegregation
discrimination
disease microorganism
disenfranchisement
dissent
divided loyalties
domestic crop

## Level 3 (cont.)

dowry
Dutch colonization
economic power
economy
Egyptian civilization
emigration
employment opportunity
English Common Law
environmental change
epic
epidemic disease
equal opportunity
equal protection of the
    laws
ethical belief
ethical systems
ethnic art
ethnic conflict
ethnic group
ethnic identity
ethnic minority
ethnic origin
evolution
exodus
extractive mining
fair employment practice
fascism
Federalist Party
feminism
feminist movement
final solution
financing
flora
foreign capital
    investment
foreign market
fortification
founders

framers
fraternal organization
French colonization
fundamental value
gender role
global communication
global market
gridiron pattern
group overlap
Haitian Revolution
hierarchy
historical account
historical fiction
historical narrative
hoarding
Holocaust
hostility
human intention
human nature
Iberia
immigration screening
imperial policy
imperialism
import
individual status
industrialization
infant mortality rate
inheritance law
innate ability
international market
international relations
interpretation
intervention
Iraq
Islamic beliefs
isolationism
jazz
Jesus Christ
Jewish monotheism
Jewish refugee

Jewish resistance
    movement
Korean War
labor force
labor union
learned behavior pattern
liberal democracy
limitations on
    government
linguistic diversity
literary narrative
long-distance migration
Lost Generation
lynching
Magna Carta (1215)
mandate
marine transportation
marital status
maritime rights
maritime technology
maritime trade route
Marshall Plan
mass consumer
    economy
matrilineal family
memento
middle-class culture
migrant worker
militant religious
    movement
military mobilization
military tactic
military unit
modern art
monarchy
monastery
monasticism
monsoon wind
moral reform
moral responsibility

## Level 3 (cont.)

moral values
mortality rate
mosque
mound builder
multiple-tier time line
mural
Muslim Empire
nation-state
national bank
national self-rule
nativism
Nazi
Nazi-Soviet Non-
    Aggression pact of
    1939
neutrality
nobility
nomadic people
North American mound-
    building people
North American plains
    society
nuclear politics
obsidian
occupational
    specialization
open range
open shop
organized labor
Paris Peace Accord of
    1973
participatory
    government
pathogen
patriarchal society
peasantry
People's Republic of
    China

Persian Gulf
perspective
philanthropist
Philippine annexation
philosophical movement
philosophy
political alliance
political border
polygamous marriage
pooled resources
port city
port of entry
Portugal
Portuguese caravel
post-World War I
post-World War II
Post Vincennes
price war
private property
private white academy
professional sector
protective tariff
Protestant Christianity
Protestant Reformation
public education
public opinion
Puritanism
racial minority
rapid industrialization
rationing
reform government
reform legislation
religious dissenter
removal policy
ritual sacrifice
Roman occupation of
    Britain
Russian absolutism
Russian Revolution of
    1917

saint
scientific method
secession
secular ruler
secular state
seed drill
segregation
semilunar calendar
separatist movement
service industry
Sicily
significant event
social agency
social attitudes
Social Darwinism
social factor
social issue
social status
Socialist Party
sovereign state
spoils system
standard of behavior
standard of living
state bureaucracy
states' rights
status
steppe lands
stereotype
stimuli
stock breeding
stratification
strike
strip mining
subculture
superpower rivalry
tariffs
telecommunication
temperance
territorial expansion
terrorism

## Level 3 (cont.)

theater of conflict
third party
totalitarian regime
trade balance
trade union
trading triangle
transformation
transmission of beliefs
transmission of culture
tribal identity
urbanization
war crime
water rights
weaponry
welfare
white-collar sector
woman suffrage
Woodrow Wilson's
   Fourteen Points
working-class culture
world history
world power
world war

## Level 4

abortion
absolutism
adaptation
affluence
African American
   community
amnesty
animal domestication
anticommunist
   movement
anti-Semitism
aristocratic power

arms embargo
arms limitations
artisan
assimilation
atomic diplomacy
autonomous power
bank recharter
barbarian
bilingual education
biological evidence
bipolar centers of power
black market
border conflict
breakup of Soviet Union
British colony
British imperialism
British monarch
capitalist country
cartography
casualty rate
Catholic clergy
centralized monarchy
chemical warfare
Chinese Communist
   Party
Christian denomination
church-state relations
city planning
civic center
class conflict
class relations
colonial rule
commodity price
common refuse
compulsory education
conscription
constitutional ideal
constitutionalism
consumer's rights
consumer culture

containment policy
contemporary life
continuity
conventional warfare
corporation
Covenant of the League
   of Nations
creditor
critical text analysis
cultural continuity
cultural identity
cultural preservation
defense policy
defense spending
demobilization
democratization
demographics
depression of 1873–1879
depression of 1893–1897
détente
diffusion
disease pandemic
distribution of powers
due process
duke
Dutch merchant class
Dutch West Indies
economy
economic dependency
economic disparity
economic reforms
educational reform
enemies of the state
energy crisis
English Parliament
entrepreneur
entrepreneurial spirit
environmental
   degradation
environmentalism

**Level 4 (cont.)**

ethical dilemma
ethnicity
evangelical argument
evangelical movement
exchange of fauna
exchange of flora
expansionism
expansionist foreign
    policy
Federalist
food plant domestication
fraud
free enterprise
free labor system
free trade
freedom of the press
fundamentalism
generational conflict
genetically determined
    behavior
genocide
geopolitics
global economy
global trade
globalizing trend
government subsidy
gradation
group identity
guerilla warfare
hearsay
hereditary social system
heredity
historical context
historical continuity
humanism
ideological conflict
ideology
imperial presidency

inalienable right to
    freedom
income gap
individualism
industrial parity
inflammatory
inflation
instinctive behavior
integration
intellectual life
internal trade
international economy
investigative technique
investment
iron metallurgy
Islamic state
Islamization
Jewish scapegoating
jihad
labor relations
legal code
liberalism
liberation theology
male-dominated job
market revolution
martyr
materialism
mercantilism
mercenary
Mexican Revolution
militarism
military-industrial
    complex
military preparedness
millennialism
mining economy
mobilization
moderate thinking
monetary policy
monotheism

mulatto
multiculturalism
multilateral aid
    organization
multinational
    corporation
Muslim country
nation building
national autonomy
national debt
national identity
national market
national security
national socialism
nationalism
Native American origin
    story
native population
natural history
neocolonialism
new scientific
    rationalism
noble savage
nonunion worker
nullification
oil crisis of 1970s
one man one vote
opposition group
oppression
outward migration
Parliament
parliamentary
    government
periodize
Philippines
Pop Art
postindustrial society
primate
prior experience
privatization

# General History | Word List

## Level 4 (cont.)

profit motive
profiteering
propaganda
propaganda campaign
property rights
Protestant clergy
province
psyche
public policy
quadrant
racial role
radicalism
rationalism
reactionary thinking
Realism
realpolitik
recession
recurrent pandemic
Red Russian
Red Scare
redistribution of wealth
refugee population
religious evangelism
reparation payment
repertoire

representative
  government
republicanism
resettlement
retaliation
reunification
rights of the disabled
rigid class
Russian Chronicle
Russian Revolution of
  1905
sanctioned country
scientific racism
second front
sectionalism
secular ideology
sedentary agriculture
self-determination
social democratization
socialism
socioeconomic group
South Africa
sovereignty
sphere of influence
stagnation of wages
staple crop production
state constitution
status quo

subsistence method
suburbanization
supply-side economics
system of alliances
traditional cultural
  identity
UN resolution
United States
  intervention
universal language
urban bourgeoisie
U.S. domestic energy
  policy
U.S. foreign policy
U.S. Smoot-Hawley
  Tariff
U.S.S.R.
Utopian community
volunteerism
wartime diplomacy
wartime inflation
welfare state
Western values
women in the clergy
workforce
world geopolitics
writ of habeas corpus

# U.S. History | Word List

## Level 2

1492
1896 election
1920s
13th Amendment
14th Amendment
15th Amendment
16th Amendment
17th Amendment
18th Amendment
19th Amendment
Age of Exploration
Alamo
Alexander Hamilton
American Expeditionary
    Force
Andrew Jackson
Antietam
Arab-Israeli crisis
Articles of
    Confederation
Axis Powers
Battle of Bull Run
Black Reconstruction
Boston
*Brown v. Board of*
    *Education* (1954)
Cabeza de Vaca
Camelot image
Cayuga
Charles Finney
Chickasaw removal
Chickasaw
Choctaw removal
coal mine strike
Confederacy
Confederate Army
Connecticut
    Compromise

Constitutional
    Convention
cotton gin
Cree removal
December 7, 1941
Democratic Party
escaped slave
European Theater
Fort Sumter
Fourteen Points
Francisco Vasquez de
    Coronado
Fredericksburg
Freedmen's Bureau
freedom ride
French Quebec
French settlement
fur trade
General Robert E. Lee
GI Bill
Golden Door
Great Awakening
Great Plains
Harlem Renaissance
Harry S. Truman
Herbert Hoover
Hispanic American
"I Have a Dream" speech
indentured servant
industrial North
internment of Japanese
    Americans
Jacqueline Kennedy
James Monroe
Jenne
Jim Bowie
Jim Crow
Jimmy Carter
John Adams
John F. Kennedy

John Hancock
King James I
Know-Nothing Party
Latino
Lexington and Concord
Louisiana
Louisiana Purchase
lower South colony
Lyndon B. Johnson
    administration
Manassas
manifest destiny
Mary McLeod Bethune
Mid-Atlantic colony
minstrel show
Missouri Compromise
Mohawk
Mormon
Mother Mary Jones
Mt. Rushmore
National Organization
    for Women
New Deal
New Federalism
New Frontier
New Jersey Plan
New Mexico
Northeast
Oneida
Onondaga
Open Door policy
Oregon
P. T. Barnum
Panama Canal
Pearl Harbor
Pennsylvania
Peter Cartwright
post-Civil War period
pre-Columbus
Prohibition

### Level 2 (cont.)

Reagan revolution
Revolutionary War
Richard Henry Lee
Richard Nixon
Ronald Reagan
Sam Houston
Samuel Adams
Santa Fe
Second Great
    Awakening
Seminole removal
Seneca
sharecropper
Shays Rebellion
Shiloh
Silent Majority
Songhai
spinning jenny
stock market crash of
    1929
suffrage movement
Supreme Court
taxation without
    representation
Texas
Texas War for
    Independence (1836)
the East
the North
the South
the West
Theodore Roosevelt
thirteen colonies
Thomas Nast
Trail of Tears
Treaty of Guadalupe
    Hidalgo
Treaty of Paris

Underground Railroad
Union Army
U.S. territory
Vicksburg
Virginia Plan
War of 1812
Warren Court
Watergate
westward expansion
Whiskey Rebellion
William H. Taft
yeoman farmer

### Level 3

1960 presidential
    campaign
African-American Union
    soldier
American dream
American foreign policy
American identity
American West
Anne Hutchinson
antebellum period
Anti-Federalist
anti-immigrant attitude
antislavery ideology
Article III of the
    Constitution
Atlantic slave trade
Bacon's rebellion
Battle for Britain
Benjamin Franklin's
    autobiography
big stick diplomacy
Calvin Coolidge
Camp David Accords
Charles Evans Hughes

Christian evangelical
    movement
Church of Jesus Christ
    of Latter-day Saints
closed shop
Compromise of 1850
Compromise of 1877
Congress
Congressional authority
Continental Congress
Dawes Severalty Act of
    1887
Declaration of
    Sentiments
Democrat
Democratic-Republican
    Party
dollar diplomacy
domestic policy
domestic program
Dr. Francis Townsend
Dred Scott decision
Dwight D. Eisenhower
Eisenhower Doctrine
election of 1800
election of 1912
*Engel v. Vitale* (1962)
English Bill of Rights
    (1689)
Equal Rights
    Amendment
Fair Deal
family assistance
    program
farm labor
featherbedding
federal Indian policy
federalism
Filipino insurrection
First Amendment

## Level 3 (cont.)

First Congress
First Lady
flawed peace
free exercise clause
French and Indian War
Garvey movement
gentleman's agreement
Glorious Revolution
Great Society
Hiram Johnson
Huey Long
impeachment
Industrial Workers of the
    World
Iranian hostage crisis
James Buchanan
James Madison
Jay's Treaty
John Marshall
Joseph McCarthy
Judiciary Act of 1789
Kennedy assassination
Ku Klux Klan
Lewis and Clark
    expedition
Little Rock 1957
Loyalist
Malcolm X
*Marbury v. Madison*
    (1803)
Massachusetts
McCarthyism
midnight judge
modern republicanism
NAACP
Navigation Acts
new freedom
new nationalism

Normandy Invasion
Northwest Ordinance of
    1787
Oregon territory
pardon of Richard Nixon
party system
Paxton Boys Massacre
Populism
Populist Party
Progressive era
Progressive movement
Reconstruction
    amendments
Republican
Republican Party
return to domesticity
Robert La Follette
Roosevelt coalition
Rust Belt
Scopes trial
Seneca Falls Convention
share the wealth
shot heard round the
    world
Soviet espionage
Sun Belt
Tenure of Office Act
thirteen virtues
Townsend Plan
Transcendentalism
trans-Mississippi region
Truman Doctrine
U.S. Supreme Court
universal white male
    suffrage
Virginia
Warren G. Harding
Whig Party
Works Progress
    Administration

WPA project

## Level 4

18th century
    republicanism
accession of Elizabeth I
affirmative action
Agricultural Adjustment
    Act
Algonkian
Alien and Sedition Acts
American Communist
    Party
American Federation of
    Labor (AFL)
Americanization
Arizona
Asian Civil Rights
    Movement
baby boom generation
Bank Recharter Bill of
    1832
Battle of Saratoga
Bay of Pigs
black legend
Carolina regulators
Carrie Chapman Catt
Chesapeake
CIO (Committee for
    Industrial Organizations)
"City Upon a Hill" speech
Civil Rights Act of 1964
Civil Works
    Administration
Civilian Conservation
    Corps
Committee for Industrial
    Organizations (CIO)

## Level 4 (cont.)

Constitution of 1787
covenant community
crabgrass frontier
crop lien system
Cross of Gold speech
*Dartmouth College v. Woodward* (1819)
D-Day
de facto segregation
de jure segregation
Democratic nominee
Desert Storm
downtown business area
East Asian Co-Prosperity Sphere
economic depression of 1819
economic depression of 1837
economic depression of 1857
election of 1960
emerging capitalist economy
Emilio Aguinaldo
European land hunger
evil empire
executive branch
farm labor movement
federal judiciary
fireside chats
First New Deal
Five Civilized Tribes
Four Freedoms speech
French Declaration of the Rights of Man
full dinner pail

Gay Liberation Movement
gay rights
General Ulysses S. Grant
General William T. Sherman
Gettysburg Address
GI Bill on higher education
*Gibbons v. Ogden* (1824)
Good Neighbor Policy
Grand Alliance
Great Migration
Greenback Labor Party
hammering campaign
Hernando Cortes
Hetch Hetchy controversy
Indian laborer
Indian Reorganization Act of 1934
International Ladies Garment Workers Union
Iran-Contra affair
James K. Polk
Japanese American
Jay Gardoqui Treaty of 1786
Jefferson Davis
John Collier
John F. Kennedy presidency
John Locke
John White
Kansas-Nebraska Act
King's Mountain
Kuwait
La Raza Unida
labor conflicts of 1894

legislative branch
Leisler's Rebellion
Lone Star Republic
mainstream America
Mark Hanna
Maryland
*McCulloch v. Maryland* (1819)
Midwest
Mississippian culture
Mormon migration to the West
mound center in Cahokia, Illinois
mound center in the Mississippi valley
National Democratic Party
National Industrial Recovery Act
National Recovery Administration
National Republican Party
National Woman Suffrage Association
New Klan
New Woman
New York City draft riots of July 1863
Northwest Territory
November 10 proposal
Old Hickory
Omaha Platform of 1892
Panama Revolution of 1903
parochial school
Peace of Paris
*Plessy v. Ferguson* (1896)

### Level 4 (cont.)

post-Cold War era
Public Works
    Administration
Quaker
Radical Republicans
relocation center
*Roe v. Wade* (1973)
Roger Williams
Roosevelt Corollary
Rural Electrification
    Administration
Sacco and Vanzetti trial
Scots-Irish

Second New Deal
secondary education
Shaysites
South Carolina
spirit of individualism
Tennessee Valley
    Authority Act
Texas Revolution
    (1836–1845)
Theodore deBry
Title VII
traditional American
    family
two-party system

Two Treatises on
    Government
Upton Sinclair
U.S. Communist Party
Victorian value
war bond
War on Poverty
War Powers Act of
    March 1942
West Indian colony
William Jennings Bryan
William McKinley
Wilmot Proviso
Zuni

## Level 2

1948 UN Declaration of Human Rights
African heritage
Afro-Eurasia
Age of Enlightenment
Alfred the Great
Americas
Andes
Arab Palestinian
Ashikaga period
Ashoka
Athenian democracy
Atlantic basin
Augustus
Australia
Aztec Empire
Aztec "Foundation of Heaven"
Baghdad
Balkans
Bartholomew de las Casas
Battle of Hastings
Benito Mussolini
Berlin blockade
Black Sea
Bombay
Boxer Rebellion
Brahmanism
Brazil
British East India Company
Buddha
Buddhism
Buenos Aires
Byzantine Empire
Byzantium
Cairo

Canton
capture of Constantinople
Carthage
cavalry warfare
celestial empire
Central Asia
Central Asian steppes
Central Iberia
Central Powers
Charlemagne
chivalry
Christian community
Christopher Columbus
Cicero
Cincinnatus
class system
Classical Greek art and architecture
clay pottery
Commodore Matthew Perry
Confucianism
Confucius
Constantine
Copernicus
Cortes' journey into Mexico
court of Heian
cowboy culture
Cro-Magnon
czar
Czar Nicholas II
daily prayer (Salat)
dharma
Diderot
discovery of diamonds
discovery of gold
Dr. Sun Yatsen
Duchy of Moscow

East Africa
Eastern Roman Empire
Edmund Cartwright
elite status
English civil war
English Revolution of 1688
Eurasia
Eurasian society
European colonial rule
European conquest
European Economic Community
European opium trade
father of modern Egypt
feudal society
founding of Rome
French East India company
French invasion of Egypt in 1798
Garibaldi
Garibaldi's nationalist redshirts
Genghis Khan
goddesses
gods
Great Canal of China
Greek city-state
Greek gods and goddesses
Guangzhou
Gupta Empire
Haitian Revolution
Hajj
Han Empire
Hebrew Torah
Hegira (Hirjah)
Hellenist culture
Hellenistic art

# World History| Word List

### Level 2 (cont.)

Henri Matisse
Hinduism
hominid
Huang He (Yellow River)
  civilization
human community
Hundred Years' War
Hungarian revolt
imperial conquest
independent lord
India
Indian Ocean
Indian spice
Indonesia
Indus Valley
industrial age
international trade
  routes
invention of paper
Ireland
Jakarta tales
James Hargreaves
James Watt
Japanese feudal society
Japanese tea ceremony
Jewish civilization
John Kay
Joseph Stalin
Julius Caesar
Justinian
Kaaba
Kilwa
King Affonso II of the
  Kongo and Po
King Alfred of England
knight
knightly class
Korea

Kush culture
Lenin
Liberty, Equality,
  Fraternity
maize cultivation
Malaysia
Mali Empire
Marcus Aurelius
Maurya empire
Mayan city-state
Mayan pyramids
Mayan religion
Mediterranean region
Meiji Japan
Mesoamerica
Mesopotamia
middle passage
Ming Dynasty
Moche civilization
modern China
Mohenjo-Daro
Mughal Empire
Muhammad
Muhammad Ali of Egypt
Mycenaean Greek
  culture
Napoleon Bonaparte
Napoleonic period
Nazi holocaust
Nazi war against the
  Jews
Neanderthal
Nero
Netherlands
New Kingdom
New Testament
New Zealand
Newton
Nile Delta
Nile Valley

Norse invasion
North Africa
Nubia
Oceania
Olmec civilization
Ottoman Empire
Pablo Picasso
Pacific Islands
Pan-Arabism
Paul the Apostle
Peru
Pharaoh
Phoenicia
Pompeii
pre-European life in the
  Americas
Qur'an/Koran
Ramadan
Rasputin
Reformation
Renaissance
Richard Arkwright
Safavid Empire
Samurai class
scientific revolution
Scipio Africanus
serf
Shah Abbas I
Shang Dynasty
Sheba
Siberia
siege of Troy
silk roads
Singapore
Socrates
Solomon
Song Dynasty
Songhai Empire
South America
South Korea

## Level 2 (cont.)

South Pacific
Southern Iberia
Soviet invasion of
    Czechoslovakia
Spanish Civil War
spice trade
Stonehenge
Sub-Saharan Africa
Suez Canal
Suleiman the
    Magnificent
Sunna
Swahili
Syria
Taj Mahal, India
Tang China
Tang Empire
Teotihuacan civilization
Tiberius Gracchus
Tigris-Euphrates Valley
Tokugawa shogunate
Tokyo
trans-Atlantic slave trade
Turkey
Turkic Empire
West Africa
Western Roman Empire
William the Conqueror
Winston Churchill
Zapotec civilization
Zheng He maritime
    expeditions
Zulu empire

## Level 3

Abbasid Empire
Abd al Quadir

African resistance
    movement
Agustin de Iturbide
Akbar
Albert Einstein
alchemy
Alfred Krupp
Algeria
Alps
American Indian nation
Ammianus Marcellinus
Anasazi
Anatolia
Andean region
apartheid
Arab Muslim
arranged marriage
Aryan culture
Ashanti
Asian art form
Assyria
Assyrian Empire
Axis country
Babylonian Empire
Baltic region
Bantu
Barbados
Berlin
Bismarck's "Blood and
    Iron" speech
Buddhist beliefs
Cape Region
Carolingian Empire
Catherine the Great
Catholic Reformation
Cecil Rhodes
Central Europe
Ceylon
Champa
Chandogya

Chandragupta
Charles Darwin
China's 1911 Republican
    Revolution
Chinese Revolution of
    1911
Christian Europe
Christian religious art
Christian soldier
classical civilization
Cleisthenes
Clothilde
Clovis
colonial Africa
commercial agriculture
Communist party in
    China
Conference of Versailles
Congress of Vienna
constitutional monarchy
Coptic Christians
courtly ideals
courtly love
creation myths of
    Babylon
creation myths of China
creation myths of Egypt
creation myths of
    Greece
creation myths of Sumer
Creole
Creole-dominated revolt
    of 1821
Crete
Crimean War
Crusades
Cultural Revolution
Dahomey
Dai Vet
Daoism/Taoism

## Level 3 (cont.)

Darius I
Darius the Great
democratic despotism
division of Germany and
    Berlin
division of the
    subcontinent
Dorothea Lange
Dutch Republic
dynastic politics
Early Middle Ages
East India Company
East Indies
Eastern Mediterranean
Elizabeth I
Ellora
Emmeline Pankhurst
empire-builder
Epic of Gilgamesh
Estates-General
Ethiopia
European imperialism
European monarchy
European resistance
    movement
fascist aggression
fascist regime
Father Miguel Hidalgo
feudal lord
feudalism
Francis Bacon
Frankish Empire
Gangetic states
Gangzhou (Canton)
Ghana
Glorious Revolution of
    1688
Gothic cathedral

Great Leap Forward
Great Plague
Great Powers in Europe
Great Reform Bill 1832
Greco-Roman antiquity
Greece
Greek art
Greek Christian
    civilization
Greek drama
Greek rationalism
Greenland
Grimke sisters
griot "keeper of tales"
Haiti
Heian
Hellenistic period
Helsinki Accords
herding societies
Hermit Kingdom
high culture
    entertainment
High Middle Ages
High Renaissance
Hittite people
Holland
Homo erectus
Homo sapiens
Ibn Battuta
Ice Age
imperial absolutism
Indian culture
Indo-Aryan people
Indo-European language
Indo-Gangetic plain
Indonesian archipelago
Inner Asia
Isfahan
Italian Renaissance
James Maxwell

Janissary Corps
Japanese modernization
Jean Jaures
Jose Clemente Orozco
Kalash church
Kamakura period
Karl Marx
karma
Kathe Kollwitz
khans
Khoisan group
kingdom of Aksum
kinship group
Kongo
Korean culture
kulak
Kuomintang
Lalibela church
lateen sails
Lenin's New Economic
    Policy
Leo Africanus
Lucretia Mott
Lunda
Macedonia
Machu Picchu
Mahdist state
Mahmud II
Malayo-Polynesia
Manchu Empire
Manchu
Mandate of Heaven
manorialism
Mao Zedong
Mao's program
Maroon society
Mauryan-Buddhist
    power
medieval Christian
    society

# World History | Word List

## Level 3 (cont.)

medieval theology
megalithic stone
    building
megalopolis
Menelik II
Meroitic period
Middle Ages
Middle Kingdom
Minoan Crete
Mohandas Gandhi
Mohandas Gandhi's call
    for nonviolent dissent
Monarch Mansa Musa
Mongol conquest of 1206
Moroccan resistance
    movement
Napoleon's invasions
Neolithic agricultural
    society
neutral nation
Newfoundland
Niger River
nirvana
North Atlantic Treaty
    Organization
Oaxaca
Old Kingdom
Old Regime France
Opium War
oracle bone inscription
Orosius
paleolithic cave painting
Panchatantra
papacy
pastoral nomadic people
Persia
Persian Empire
Peter Stolypin

Peter the Great
Pizarro
Poland
polis
Polynesia
post-Mao China
Priscus
Punic Wars
Queen Hatshepsut
Quin Empire
Ramsay MacDonald
Ramses II
Raymond Poincaré
Reagan-Gorbachev
    summit diplomacy
reconquest of Spain
reincarnation
Renaissance humanism
René Descartes
Robert Owen's New
    Lanark System
Roman Catholic Church
Romanticism
Rosa Luxemburg
royal court
Rule of St. Benedict
Samarkand
Samori Ture
Sassanid Empire
Saudi Arabia
Saxon peoples
Scythian society
second industrial
    revolution
seizure of
    Constantinople
Selim III
Shiba Kokan
Shinto
Svetaketu

Siam
Sigmund Freud
Solon
Sotabu screen
South Asia
Soviet bloc
Soviet domination
Soviet invasion of
    Afghanistan
Spanish Muslim society
squire
St. Petersburg, "window
    on the west"
Stalin's purge
Stanley Baldwin
story of Olaudah
    Equiano (Gustavus
    Vassa)
Sudan
the Gracchi
three piece iron
Thutmose III
Tiananmen Square
    protest
Timur the Lame
    (Tamerlane)
Tippu Tip
Toltecs
Torah
Toussaint L'Ouverture
trench warfare
trial of Galileo
Trojan war
Turkic migration
Turkestan
unification of Germany
unification of Italy
United States foreign
    policy
Upanishad

**Building Academic Vocabulary** | Teacher's Manual

## Level 3 (cont.)

U.S. isolationist policy
Vedas
Vedic gods
warrior culture
Warsaw Pact
West Asia
Western and Eastern
    European societies
Western art and
    literature
Western culture
White Sea
Xiongnu society
Zagwé Dynasty
Zanzibar
Zhou Dynasty
Zhu Xi

## Level 4

1994 Cairo Conference
    on World Population
Abdul-Mejid
aboriginal population
absolutist state
Abstract Expressionism
Adam Smith
Aegean region
African nationalist
    movement
African village life
Akbar Islam
Akhenaton (Amenhotep
    IV)
al-Afghani
Alexander
Alexander of Macedon
alphabetic writing

Amsterdam
Angkor Wat
Anglo-Saxon Boniface
Arab Caliphate
Arab League
Arabia
Arabic
Argentina
Aristotle
art of courtly love
Ataturk
Athens
atonism
Austria
Austro-Hungarian
    Empire
Babylon
Balfour Declaration
Battle of Tours of 733
Bavaria
Bhati movement
biblical account of
    Genesis
Bismarck
Black Death
Black Legend
Bloody Sunday
Boccaccio
Boer
Boer War
Bolshevik
Brazilian independence
    movement
Britain's modernizing
    policy in India
British West Indies
Brooke
Bruges
Buddhist-Hindu culture
Buddhist monk

Buganda
Byzantine church
Cambodia
Caspian Sea
cassava
Caucasus
caudillo
Cavalier
Cavour
Charter Oath of 1868
Chartist movement
Chile
Chimu society
China's population
    growth
China's revolutionary
    movement
Chinese workers
Chinese writing system
Christian missionary
Christian monotheism
city-state
Code Napoléon
code of Hammurabi
Conference at San Remo
Constantinople
cremation of Strasbourg
    Jews
Cubism
Cuzco
Cyrus I
Czar Nicholas I
Dadaism
Damascus
David Siqueiros
Decembrist uprising
Declaration of the Rights
    of Man
Declaration of the Rights
    of Women

## Level 4 (cont.)

Descartes' *Discourse on Method*
*Diary of Murasaki Shikibu*
Diego Rivera
Diem regime
Dreyfus affair
early modern society
Emperor Aurangzeb
Ems telegram
enclosure movement
encomienda system
Enlightened Despot
Enuma Elish
Erich Remarque
Ernest Hemingway
Ethiopian art
Ethiopian rock churches
Eurasian empire
European country
European Jew
European manorial system
Existentialism
Expressionism
expulsion of Jews and Muslims from Spain
foot binding
forced collectivization
Franco-Prussian War
French Estates-General
French salon
French West Indies
Freud's psychoanalytic method
Geneva Accords
Genoa
gentry elite

George Orwell
German concept of Kultur
German Empire
German Federal Republic
Germanic peoples
Ghaznavid Empire
Golden Horde
Great Khan Mongke
Great Khan Ogodei
Great War
Great Western Schism
Greek comedy
Greek Orthodox Christianity
Greek philosopher
Greek tragedy
Guatemala
guild
hacienda
Hadith
Hapsburg Empire
Hatt-I-Humayun
Heian period
Herodotus
hominid community
Hun invasions
Hung-wu emperor
Iberian Empire
*Iliad*
imperial Mughal
Impressionism
Indian concept of ideal kingship
Indian uprising of 1857
Iran
Ismail
Italian humanism
Jamal al-Din

Japanese invasion of China
Jenn-jeno
Jewish and Arab inhabitants of Palestine
Jewish diaspora
Jewish flight to Poland and Russia
Jiang Jieshi
Joan of Arc
John of Plano Carpini
Joseph Francois Dupleix's theory of "divide and rule"
Joseph II
Kan
Kangzi emperor
Kashmir
Kerensky
Kievan Russia
King Joao II
Kumbi-Saleh
Latin
Latin American revolution
Latin Catholic church
Lenin's ideology
lingua franca
Lord Dalhousie
Louis XIV
Machiavelli
Magyar cavalry
*Mahabharata*
Mahdi Muhammad Ahmad I
Maratha
Marx and Engel's *Communist Manifesto*

## Level 4 (cont.)

Marxism
May Fourth movement
Mayan "Long Count" calendar
Mediterranean Empire
*Mein Kampf*
Mesolithic
mestizo
Mudejar Muslim
Munich Agreement in 1938
Nazi genocide
Nazi ideology
Nazi-Soviet Non-Aggression Pact, 1939
neo-Confucianism
Neolithic revolution
New England colony
New Granada
New World
nineteenth-century literature
Noh drama
Nok terra cotta figure
nonhominid
northern Italian city-state
October Manifesto
*Odyssey*
Olympia de Gouge
one child policy in China
Orthodox Christianity
Pallavas
Pandyas
Pan-Slavism
partition of Africa
Pax Mongolica
Plato

Plato's *Republic*
poetry of Kabir
poetry of Mirabai
pogroms in the Holy Roman Empire
Polish rebellion
Popul Vuh
pre-industrial England
principle of the "Invisible Hand"
process of Russification
Protestant Work Ethic
Qianlong emperor
Qing position on opium
Qizilbash nomadic tribesmen
Rabbinic Judaism
Ram Mohan Roy
*Ramayana*
Rashid Rida
Red Sea
regulated family and community life
Romanization of Europe
Roundhead
royal patronage
Rudyard Kipling's "White Man's Burden"
Sahara desert
sans-culottes
Sargon
Schlieffen Plan
Seljuk Empire
Sikh
Sino-Japanese War
Slavic world
Socialist Realism
South African (Anglo-Boer) War
South India

Southern Africa
Southern Europe
Soviet non-aggression pact
Spender
Srivijaya
Stalinist totalitarianism
Strait of Malacca
Sufism
Sui dynasty
Sumeria
Sun Yatsen
Sunni and Shi'ite factions
Surrealism
Sykes-Picot Agreement
Taiping Rebellion
temple of Madurai
temporary dominance
Thailand
the Congo
The Interesting Narrative of the Life of Olaudah Equiano
the Netherlands
*The Pillow Book* by Sei Shonagon
*The Prince* by Machiavelli
*The Wealth of Nations*
Teotihuacan
Tiahuanaco society
Trans-Siberian railroad
Treaty of Nanking (1842)
Treaty of Shimonoseki (1895)
Treaty of Versailles
Ukraine
Umayyad Dynasty
"unified" India

**Level 4 (cont.)**

Venice
Viking longboat
Vladimir of Kiev
Western hegemony

Western political thought
White Paper Reports on
    Palestine
White Russian
world influenza
    pandemic 1918–1919

Young Turk movement
Yuan Dynasty
Zionist Movement
Zoroastrianism

# Geography | Word List

### Level 1

airport
America
area
barrier
body of water
California
city
city park
climate
climate change
coast
cold climate
community
community project
competition
construction
country
creek
crop
custom
dam
desert
direction
distance
downtown
elevation
exploration
factory
family
farming
fishing
flood
forest
fuel
globe
government
graph
highway

hill
home
hospital
hotel
housing
lake
land
local community
location
map
measurement
mile
mountain
museum
nation
neighborhood
ocean
park
pattern
pipeline
place
plant population
population
position
railroad
rainfall
region
river
road
rural region
seasons
settlement
shelter
ship
shopping center
soil
sports stadium
state
stream
temperature

timber
town
transportation
United States
urban area
vegetation
village
weather
wildlife
world
yard size

### Level 2

accessibility
aerial photograph
Africa
agricultural practice
agriculture
air conditioning
air pollution
Alaska
Antarctic Circle
Appalachian Mountains
Arizona
artifacts
Asia
atmosphere
billboards
boomtown
boundary
Canada
capacity
capital
cardinal direction
central business district
chart
city center
civil war

## Level 2 (cont.)

coal mining
coastal area
colonization
Colorado mining town
    (19th century)
communication route
conservation issue
contagious disease
continent
county
crop failure
crop yield
cultural tradition
culture
culture group
discovery
Dominican Republic
downwind
drought
earthquake
Earth-sun relation
East Asia
East Coast
economic region
education system
energy consumption
England
environment
environmental
    conditions
equator
erosion
Europe
European colonialism
expansion
fall line
famine
farmland

fast-food restaurant
fertile soil
fire station
flash flood
food chain
food supply
food web
force
forest cover
forest fire
forestry
fossil fuel
France
Ganges River Valley
ghost town
grassland
harbor
Hindus
historic site
history of oil discovery
holy city
houses on stilts
humid tropical climate
Indian Ocean
inhabitants
International Date Line
invasion
iron
iron ore
irrigation
Japan
kilometer
land clearing
land use
land use regulation
landform
landlocked country
landmark
landscape
latitude

legend
life cycle
life expectancy
lifestyle
local water
logging
longitude
Louisiana
manufacturing plant
map grid
map projection
marketplace
metropolitan area
Mexico
mineral resource
mining
mining area
Mississippi River
monsoon
mountain pass
mountain range
mud slide
Muslim trading vessel
national capital
national forest
Native Americans
natural disaster
natural hazard
New Jersey
North America
North Pole
nuclear power plant
ocean current
Pacific rim
parallel
Pennsylvania
physical feature
place of origin
plain
plantation

## Level 2 (cont.)

plantation agriculture
plateau
plot
pollution
port
port city
precinct
precipitation
preservation
projection
province
rain forest
recreation area
recycling
refrigerated railroad car
refrigerated trucking
reusable
river system
Riyadh
road development
Ruhr
running water
Russia
satellite image
scale
scarce resource
scenic area
school attendance zone
section
single household
site
situation
smog
social class
society
soil conservation
soil region
solar energy

South
South America
South Pole
Spain
storage
style of homes
suburban area
technology
territory
Texas
timber cutting
time zone
topographic map
tornado
tourist center
township
trade pact
trade route
trade wind
transportation route
transportation system
vegetation region
volcano
volume
water availability
water basin
water crossing
water pollution
waterway
West Coast
wetland
wind storm
windward

## Level 3

acid rain
adaptation
Algeria

alphanumeric system
alternative energy
    source
Amsterdam
architectural style of
    buildings
arid climate
assimilation
Australia
average family size
axis
barrier island
Belgium
bicycle lane
biome
biosphere
Boston
boundary dispute
Brenner Pass
building style
Burma Pass
Canberra
Capitol Hill
central place
cheap labor
Chile
China
Chinatown
Chinese textile
clearing of forest
climate region
Congo
conservationist
contemporary system of
    communication
Cumberland Gap
data set
database
decentralization
Delaware River

## Level 3 (cont.)

demographic change
demographic information
density
density of population
developed country
developing country
diamond trade
diesel machinery
dispersion
division (of Earth's
    surface)
downstream
drainage basin
dry-land farming
    technique
earth-moving machinery
earthquake-resistant
    construction
earthquake zone
economic alliance
ecosystem
electric car
energy-poor region
energy industry
energy source
equilibrium
Ethiopia
ethnic composition
evacuation route
Everglades
export
fall line of the
    Appalachians
fauna
feeding level
flat-map projection
flood-control project
floodplain

flora
fungi
Gateway Arch (St. Louis)
geographic factor
global impact
global warming
Golden Gate Bridge (San
    Francisco)
Great American Desert
grid
hemisphere
historic preservation
Hong Kong
housing development
Huang Ho
human process
hurricane
hurricane shelter
hurricane tracks
hydroelectric power
imported resource
Indians
Indonesia
industrial center
industrial district
infant mortality rate
infrastructure
interdependence
internal structure
Inuit
involuntary migration
Iraq invasion of Kuwait
    (1991)
Irish immigrant
isthmus
Italy
Jamaican sugar
Japanese occupation of
    Manchuria (1930s)
Khyber Pass

landlocked
land-use data
land-use pattern
language region
leeward
levee
life form
linkage
literacy rate
lithosphere
Little Italy
local scale
major parallel
marine climate
marine vegetation
meridian
Mesopotamia
midaltitude
migrant population
military campaign
military installation
mobility
Moslems
multiculturalism
nationalism
natural resource
natural vegetation
natural wetlands
Netherlands
New Delhi
Nile Valley
nitrogen cycle
nonrenewable resource
nuclear-waste storage
ocean circulation
ocean pollution
Ogallala Aquifer
old-growth forest
Opera House (Sydney,
    Australia)

## Level 3 (cont.)

origin
overfishing
overpopulation
Pakistan
paper factory
pedestrian walkway
pesticide
petroleum
Philippine archipelago
Philippines
physical environment
physical geography
physical variation
plant species
political region
political unit
population
    concentration
population density
population distribution
population growth rate
population region
population structure
postal zone
prevailing wind
prime meridian
    (Greenwich meridian)
principal line
principal meridians
production site
public housing
public transit
raw material
recession
reforestation
region of contact
regional boundary
regrowth

religious facility
renewable resource
residential pattern
resource management
ridge-and-valley pattern
Riviera
runoff
rust belt
satellite-based communi-
    cations system
Saudi Arabia
savanna
school district
sea wall
seasonal pattern of life
semiarid area
settlement pattern
shifting civilization
Siberia
Sikhs
Singapore
single-industry city
soil erosion
soil fertility
solar power
South Africa
Soviet Union
spatial
spatial arrangement
spatial perception
spatial scale
spread of bubonic
    plague
spread of disease
standard of living
steel-tipped plow
strait
strip mining
suburbanization
Sunbelt

system
Tacoma Strait
tariff
technological hazard
telephone area code
temperature fluctuation
terrace
terraced rice fields
The Hague
thematic map
topography
Tower Bridge (London)
trade advantage
transportation hub
Trenton
triangular trade route
Tropic of Cancer
Tropic of Capricorn
tropical rain forest
truck-farming community
tsunami
tundra
Twin Peaks (San
    Francisco)
urban commuting
use of explosives
Vietnamese
voluntary migration
Washington
water spring
water supply
watershed
work animal
World Court
Yucatan Peninsula

## Level 4

absolute location

# Geography | Word List

## Level 4 (cont.)

acculturation
agribusiness
agricultural soil
AIDS
airborne emission
air-mass circulation
alluvial fan
Americentric
aquifer
artesian wells
atmospheric pressure
    cells
atmospheric warming
Basque minority
Bible Belt
biodiversity
biological magnification
British Empire
bubonic plague
Buddhism
Burkina Faso
carbon cycle
Caribbean Basin
Carolingian Empire
carrying capacity
cartogram
cartographer
census data
census district
center-pivot irrigation
Central Europe
central place theory
chemical cycle
chemical fertilizer
Chernobyl nuclear
    accident
choropleth map
circuit-court district

climate graph
    (climagraph)
coastal ecosystem
coastal flood zone
command economy
commodity flow
Common Market
comparative advantage
complementarity
concentrated settlement
    form
concentration of
    services
concentric zone model
congressional district
container company
contaminant
contemporary economic
    trade network
continental climate
continental drift
cost-distance
crude birth rate
crude death rate
cultural diffusion
cultural landscape
culture hearth
culture region
cycling of energy
decolonization
deforestation
demographic transition
demography
depleted rain forests of
    central Africa
deposition
desertification
diffusion
diffusion of tobacco
    smoking

distance decay
distribution of
    ecosystems
doubling time
drought-plagued Sahel
dust storm
dynamic system
eastern Australia
eastern United States
ecology
economic dominance
economic incentive
economically developing
    nation
edge city
environmental
    degradation
environmental
    determinism
equinox
erosional agent
ethnic elitism
ethnic enclave
ethnic minority
ethnicity
ethnocentrism
Eurocentric
European Union
eutrophication
exurban area
facsimile transmission
    service
fanshed
feedback loop
fertility rate
flow map
flow of energy
flow pattern
flow resource
flowchart

# Geography | Word List

## Level 4 (cont.)

foreign capital
foreign market
formal region
free-trade zone
French colonization of
    Indochina
friction
friction of distance
functional region
gentrification
Geographic Information
    Systems (GIS)
geographic technology
geomorphology
GIS (Geographic
    Information Systems)
global market
global migration pattern
Great Barrier Reef
Great Plains Dust Bowl
greenhouse effect
greenway
Gross Domestic Product
Gross National Product
groundwater quality
groundwater reduction
habitat destruction
Han dynasty
hazardous waste
    handling
health care facility
High Plains
high-latitude place
hinterland
hub-and-spoke
human adaptation
human control over
    nature

human-induced change
Hutus
hybridization of crops
hydrilla
hydrologic cycle
hydrosphere
indigenous people
Industrial Revolution
industrialization
intermediate directions
international debt crisis
interstate highway
    system
intervening opportunity
introduction of species
Iran
Iraq
Jerusalem
Kurds
lake desiccation
lake ecosystem
land degradation
landform relief
land value
landmass
land-survey system
Latin America
law of retail gravitation
life experience
light-rail system
location principle
Malaysian rain forest
market economy
megalopolis
mental map
mercantilism
metropolitan corridor
microclimate
midlatitude forest
migration counterstream

migration stream
molybdenum
monoculture
moraine
multinational
    organization
municipality
NAFTA
nation-state
natural population
    increase
network
Nicaragua
North Korea
Nova Scotia
oblate spheroid
ocean ecosystem
Ontario
OPEC
overcutting of pine
    forest
oxygen cycle
ozone depletion
ozone layer
perceptual region
peripheral area
petroleum consumption
phosphate reserves
physical process
physiography
physiological population
    density
planned city
plant community
plate tectonics
population pyramid
Portuguese
post-reunification
    Germany
power bloc

## Level 4 (cont.)

primary data
primary economic
    activity
primate city
principal parallels
profitability
pull factors
push factors
racial minority
rain shadow
rate of natural increase
rate of resource
    consumption
reduction of species
    diversity
regional planning district
regionalization
relative humidity
relative location
religious ties
relocation strategy
remote sensing
resource base
Ring of Fire
Roman Empire
rural-to-urban migration
rutile sand
Rwanda
salinization
salt accumulation
sand movement

secondary economic
    activity
sector model
sediment
seismic activity
sequence occupance
silting
Sinocentric
Social Security number
social welfare of
    workers
socioeconomic status
soil acidification
soil creep
soil salinization
solar radiation
South Korea
Southeast Asia
Spanish settlement
stage of life
statutory requirement
sub-Arctic environment
sub-Saharan Africa
subsistence agriculture
subsistence farming
sustainable development
sustainable environment
synergy
systemic
tectonic plate
tectonic process
tertiary economic
    activity

the Pampas in Argentina
theory of comparative
    advantage
thermal
threshold
threshold population
tidal process
toxic dumping
toxic waste handling
transnational
    corporation
transportation corridor
transregional alliance
travel effort
tropical soil degradation
tungsten
Turkey
Tutsis
Ukraine
urban heat island
urban morphology
urbanization
volcanism
voting ward
ward
weathering
wilderness area
world atmospheric
    circulation
world temperature
    increase
zoned use of land
zoning regulation

# Civics | Word List

## Level 1

accept responsibility for
   one's actions
agreement
authority
citizen
control
duty
education
election
flag
good law
good rule
government
honesty
individual
justice
law
leader
nation
national anthem
official
open-mindedness
order
Pledge of Allegiance
police authority
power
privacy
qualifications
race
religion
respect for law
respect for the rights of
   others
responsibility
rights
rule
school
symbol

take turns
territory
trade
transportation
truth
United States
volunteer
vote
war

## Level 2

absence of rules and
   laws
abuse of power
alien
American holiday
American society
benefits
Bill of Rights
campaign
candidate
Chamber of Commerce
citizenship
city council
civic responsibility
civic-mindedness
clean air laws
Columbus Day
common good
community
compromise
Congress
consent of the governed
consider the rights and
   interests of others
courts
Declaration of
   Independence

democracy
diplomacy
discrimination
discrimination based on
   age
discrimination based on
   disability
discrimination based on
   ethnicity
discrimination based on
   gender
discrimination based on
   language
discrimination based on
   religious belief
diversity
elected representative
equal opportunity
equal pay for equal work
evidence
executive branch
Fourth of July
freedom of religion
freedom of speech
geographical
   representation
governor
great seal
Greek democracy
health services
highest law of the land
human rights
individual liberty
individual responsibility
individual rights
invasion of privacy
jury duty
Labor Day
labor union
law enforcement

# Civics | Word List

## Level 2 (cont.)

lawmaker
leadership
legislator
liberty and justice for all
life, liberty, and the
    pursuit of happiness
local government
Martin Luther King Jr.
mayor
Memorial Day
military force
military intervention
national origin
national park
national security
negotiation
nobility
oath of office
patriotism
peaceful demonstration
personal responsibility
petition
political candidate
political office
political party
politics
pollution
population growth
poverty
prejudice
president
presidential election
Presidents Day
privilege
P.T.A.
public good
public office
public policy

public servant
public utilities
pure food and drug laws
quality of life
racial discrimination
racial diversity
reform
refugee
religious belief
religious discrimination
representation
representative
revolution
right to a fair trial
right to choose one's
    work
right to criticize the
    government
right to join a political
    party
right to public education
right to vote
royalty
rule by the people
rule of law
school board
school prayer
self-discipline
self-governance
senator
slavery
special interest group
state government
state legislature
state senator
Statue of Justice
Statue of Liberty
Supreme Court
taxes
Thanksgiving

trade agreement
treaty
tribal council
tribal government
Uncle Sam
unemployment
United States citizenship
United States
    Constitution
unlimited government
value
Veterans Day
volunteerism
welfare
world leader

## Level 3

AFL-CIO
Aid to Families with
    Dependent Children
allegiance
ambassador
American citizenship
American Revolution
American tribal
    government
armed forces service
arms control
bias
binding agreement
cabinet
capital punishment
central government
charitable group
citizenship by birth
civil rights
civil rights movement

# Civics | Word List

## Level 3 (cont.)

civilian control of the military
coining money
colonial charters
commander in chief
Common Cause
Confederate States of America
conflict management
constitutional law
corrective justice
covert action
criminal law
curfew
customs search
death penalty
debate
delegated powers
demographics
demonstration
domestic policy
dress code
due process
economic aid
economic incentive
economic sanctions
economic security
English Parliament
enumerated powers
Environmental Protection Act
environmental protection movement
equal justice for all
equal protection of the law
equal rights under the law

equity
ethical dilemma
ethnic diversity
ex post facto
executive power
fair notice of a hearing
fair trial
federal court
federal income tax
First Amendment
foreign aid
foreign policy
foreign relations
form a more perfect union
Founders
Framers
freedom of assembly
freedom of association
freedom of conscience
freedom of petition
freedom of press
freedom of residence
freedom to emigrate
freedom to marry whom one chooses
freedom to travel freely
French Revolution
fundamental principles of American democracy
gender diversity
general election
Gettysburg Address
Greenpeace
gun control
habeas corpus
hate speech
immigration
impeachment

income tax
indentured servitude
informed citizenry
institution (political)
interest group
international law
International Red Cross
interstate commerce
interstate highways
judicial branch
judicial power
just compensation
juvenile
labor movement
landmark decision
Latin America
League of Women Voters
legal recourse
legislative branch
legislative power
legislature
letter to the editor
licensing
limited government
local election
lower court
loyal opposition
majority rule
*Marbury v. Madison* (1803)
Martin Luther King Jr.'s "I Have a Dream" speech
Mayflower Compact
Medicaid
Medicare
minimum wage
minority rights
NAACP
national defense

## Level 3 (cont.)

nation-state
NATO
naturalization
Nineteenth Amendment
nomination
OAS
Parliament
parliamentary system
People's Republic of
  China
picket
political life
political appointment
popular sovereignty
prayer in public school
preamble
Preamble to the
  Constitution
president's cabinet
presumption of
  innocence
prime minister
principle
private life
private property
property tax
protest
public agenda
public life
public opinion poll
public trial
Pure Food and Drug Act
recall election
representative
  democracy
representative
  government
revenue

right of appeal
right to acquire/dispose
  of property
right to copyright
right to counsel
right to enter into a
  lawful contract
right to equal protection
  of the law
right to establish a
  business
right to hold public
  office
right to join a labor
  union
right to join a
  professional
  association
right to know
right to patent
right to privacy
right to property
Roman Republic
rule of men
Senate
separation of church and
  state
separation of powers
shared power
Sixteenth Amendment
slander
Social Security
sovereign state
sovereignty
speedy trial
state constitution
state court
state election
state sales tax
state sovereignty

states' rights
suffrage
suffrage movement
Supreme Being
tariff
tax revenue
terrorism
The Federalist Papers
the press
totalitarian system
treason
trial by jury
union
United Nations
United Nations Charter
Universal Declaration of
  Human Rights
*U.S. v. Nixon* (1974)
veto power
Virgin Islands
vote of no confidence
voter registration
World Council of
  Churches
World Court

## Level 4

abortion
adversary system
advice and consent
affirmative action
"all men are created
  equal"
allocation of power
American constitutional
  democracy
Americans with
  Disabilities Act

# Civics | Word List

## Level 4 (cont.)

Amnesty International
anarchy
Antarctic Treaty
Anti-Federalist
arbitrary rule
arbitration
Article I of the
    Constitution
Article I, Section 7
Article I, Section 8
Article II of the
    Constitution
Article III of the
    Constitution
Articles of
    Confederation
authoritarian system
bilateral agreement
body politic
boycott
bribery
British constitution
*Brown v. Board of
    Education* (1954)
bureaucracy
capricious rule
caste system
charter local
    government
chauvinism
checks and balances
Chief Joseph's "I Shall
    Fight No More
    Forever"
Chinese Revolution
citizenry
citizens and subjects
civil disobedience

civil law
civil liberties
civil rights legislation
Civil War amendments
civilian review board
civility
class boundaries
class system
"clear and present
    danger" rule
Cold War
collective decision
common law
communism
Communist International
concurrent power
congressional district
congressional election
conservative
constituency
Constitutional
    amendment
constitutional
    democracy
constitutionalism
constitutionality of laws
consumer product safety
copyright
cruel and unusual
    punishment
democratic legislature
Democratic Party
direct democracy
direct popular rule
distribution of power
divine law
divine right
domestic tranquility
double jeopardy
E Pluribus Unum

electoral system
eminent domain
English Bill of Rights
Enlightenment
equal protection clause
Equal Rights
    Amendment
established religion
establishment clause
estate tax
ethnicity
European Union
excise tax
exclusionary rule
Federal
    Communications
    Commission
Federal Reserve
federal supremacy
    clause
federalism
Federalist
Food and Drug
    Administration
Fourteenth Amendment
franchise
free enterprise
free exercise clause
freedom to choose
    employment
freedom to enter into
    contracts
fundamental rights
GATT
general welfare
general welfare clause
Head Start
Helsinki Accord
higher court review
House of Commons

# Civics | Word List

### Level 4 (cont.)

House of Lords
humanitarian aid
ideology
illegal search and seizure
immigration policy
impartial tribunal
imperial power
inalienable rights
incorporation
independent judiciary
independent regulatory
    agency
International Monetary
    Fund
jingoism
judicial review
junta
jurisdiction
legislation
legislative districting
legitimacy
libel
liberal
liberalism
Lincoln's "House Divided"
litigation
lobbying
Magna Carta
market economy
Marshall Plan
monarchy
Monroe Doctrine
moral obligation
Most Favored Nation
    Agreements
multilateral agreement
multinational
    corporation

NAFTA
National Education
    Association
national interest
nationalism
natural law
natural rights
Ninth Amendment
Northwest Ordinance
op-ed page
Organization of
    American States
organized crime
organized labor
patent
perjury
personal autonomy
political cartoon
political culture
political efficacy
political ideology
political philosophy
political rights
popular will
power of the purse
power to declare war
primary election
private domain
private sector
proportional system
Protestant Reformation
Puritan ethic
referendum
republic
Republican Party
reserved power
right to due process of
    law
right to life
school voucher

scope and limit
search and seizure
self-determination
self-evident truths
service group
sexual harassment
social contract
social equity
social issue
social welfare
Sojourner Truth's "Ain't I
    a Woman?"
state bill of rights
statute law
supremacy clause
system of checks and
    balances
Tenth Amendment
term limitation
third party
time, place, manner
    restrictions
two-party system
unenumerated rights
UNICEF
union movement
unitary government
urban decay
urban riot
vigilantism
warrant
"We the People . . ."
winner-take-all system
Woodrow Wilson's
    "Fourteen Points"
World Bank
World War I
World War II
zoning

# Economics | Word List

### Level 1

advertising
bank
business
buyer
coin
cost
debt
dime
dollar
earn
goods
job
labor
loss
money
needs
penny
poverty
price
quarter
sale
save
sell
seller
services
skills
spending
wants
worker

### Level 2

advantage
barter
benefit
borrow
business firm
capital

capital goods
capital resource
competition
competitive market
consumer
consumption
contract
contract negotiation
credit
currency
customer service
division of labor
earnings
economy
employer
employment
entrepreneur
firm
funds
goods/services exchange
household
incentive
income
income tax
innovation
invention
investment
investor
limited budget
limited resources
loan
market
natural resource
partnership
payment
penalty
price decrease
price increase
producer
product

profit
profit opportunity
purchasing power
rent
resource
resource scarcity
revenue
reward
risk
salary
savings
scarcity
shortage
specialization
surplus
tax
trade
trade barrier
trade-off
training
value
wage

### Level 3

average price level
carrying money
central authority
checking account
command economic
    system
commercial bank
contract labor
cost of production
credit policy
decentralization
disincentive
earned income
economic incentive

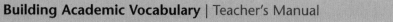

# Economics | Word List

### Level 3 (cont.)

economic indicator
economic specialization
equilibrium
exchange rate
export
exporting firm
finance
foreign exchange market
foreign trade
free trade
fringe benefit
full-time employment
funding
Gross Domestic Product
human capital
human resource
import
inflation
inflation rate
interest
intermediary
labor force
labor market
labor union
large firm
law of supply and
  demand
market clearing price
market economy
market exchange
national defense
  spending
national economy
negative incentive
nonprofit organization
nonrival product
opportunity benefit
opportunity cost

output per hour
output per machine
output per unit of land
output per worker
part-time employment
positive incentive
private market
production
productivity
property rights
public project
quota
relative price
rent control
risk reduction
sales tax
savings account
self-employment
self-sufficiency
shared consumption
side effect
special interest group
specialized economic
  institution
standard currency
standard of living
storing money
substitute product
supplier
surcharge
system of weights and
  measures
tax deduction
tax exemption
tax reduction
total benefit
total cost
total market value
unemployment
unemployment rate

wage rate
work rule

### Level 4

absolute advantage
aggregate demand
aggregate supply
allocation method
bait and switch
balanced budget
budget constraint
budget deficit
budget surplus
business deduction
capital stock
capitalism
circulation of money
collective bargaining
collusion
communism
comparative advantage
complementary product
consumer fraud
Consumer Price Index
consumer spending
consumer tastes
cooperative
corporate spending
cost-benefit ratio
cost-push inflation
current interest rate
cyclical unemployment
default on a loan
deferment of loan
deficit
deflation
demand-pull inflation
demand curve

# Economics | Word List

**Level 4 (cont.)**

depression
deregulation
discount rate
disposable income
Dow Jones
durable goods
economic risk
economic theory
economics
elasticity
expected rate of
    inflation
expenditure
externalities
Federal Reserve System
federal spending
federal tax revenue
financial institution
fiscal policy
fixed income
fixed rate of interest
free enterprise
frictional employment
frictional unemployment
functional distribution of
    income
government directive
government employee
government security
government spending
grant
home office
income distribution
incorporation
interest payment
interest rate
labor force immobility
large-scale investment

liability rules
macroeconomics
marginal benefit
marginal cost
marketplace
maximum employment
medical coverage
medical expenditure
microeconomics
monetary policy
money supply
monopoly
national debt
national government
    spending
natural monopoly
negative externality
net export
nominal Gross Domestic
    Product
nominal interest rate
nondurable goods
nonexclusion
nonprice competition
oligopoly
open market purchase
payroll tax
per capita GDP
personal distribution of
    income
personal income
physical capital
positive externality
prevailing price
price ceiling
price control
price floor
price stability
private investment
    spending

production cost
production method
production output
property tax
proprietor's income
public service
    commission
public welfare
public works
real cost
real GDP
real interest rate
recession
redistribution of income
regulation
rental income
research and
    development
reserve requirement
return on investment
seasonal unemployment
service charge
shareholder
shift in demand curve
shift in supply curve
social security
social security
    withholding
socialism
speculation
standard measure (of
    unemployment rate)
standard measures
standard weights
state revenue
stock
stock market
stockholder
structural
    unemployment

# Economics | Word List

**Level 4 (cont.)**

subsidy
supply curve
tariffs
tax revenue

telecommuting
transaction cost
transfer payment
transportation cost
underground economy
virtual company

Wall Street
warranty
work experience
workers' compensation

# Health | Word List

## Level 1

911
abuse
argument
birth
bleeding
blood
bruise
conflict
congestion
cough
cut
death
dentist
diet
disease
divorce
doctor
drug
emergency
exercise
extended family
family member
fat
feelings
feelings of others
fever
fire safety
food group
food handling
gums
hand washing
harmful substance
health
helmet
hospital
human body
illness
injury

listening skill
marriage
medicine
nails
name calling
nurse
paramedic
police officer
pollution
precaution
rash
rest
risk
safety rule
scratch
simple injury
skin
stranger
symptom
tooth decay
traffic safety
water safety
wheezing

## Level 2

acne
activity level
alcohol
calorie
cooking temperature
dental floss
dietitian
disability
drug abuse
early detection and
    treatment
environment
exercise program

fiber
first- (second-, third-)
    degree burn
first aid
food label
growth cycle
health goal
health screening
healthy relationship
HMO
infant
infectious disease
lifestyle
medical personnel
medication
minor burn
mood swing
mouth guard
neighborhood safety
nonprescription drug
nonviolent conflict
resolution
nutritional value
obesity
old age
over-the-counter
    medicine
overeating
parenthood
peer pressure
personal health goal
physical fitness
physician
poison
pregnancy
prescription medicine
protective equipment
psychological health
puberty
public health clinic

# Health | Word List

## Level 2 (cont.)

recreation safety
refusal skill
responsibility
self-control
sexual abuse
sexual maturation
smoking
social pressure
spoiled food
stress
stress management
sunscreen
tobacco abuse
treatment
voice change
warning label
weight gain
weight loss
well-being

## Level 3

abdominal thrust
   maneuver
adolescence
adolescent
   independence
alcohol abuse
American Heart
   Association
American Lung
   Association
anemia
anorexia
asthma
bacteria
body system
bulimia

cancer
cardiopulmonary
   resuscitation
chronic disease
community agency
community health
conception
conflict resolution
counseling
CPR
cultural belief
denial
dental health
depression
diabetes
Diabetes Association
discrimination
domestic violence
drug-seeking behavior
drug dependency
drunk and drugged
   driving
eating disorder
emergency plan
emotional abuse
emphysema
family history
food additive
food refrigeration
food storage
handicapping condition
health-care provider
health fad
health risk
heart disease
Heimlich maneuver
hygiene
immunization
injury-prevention
   strategy

long-term consequence
lung cancer
malnutrition
maturation
mental health clinic
mental health
neglect
negotiation skill
other-directed violence
personal health
   assessment
personal hygiene
plaque
pollutant
prejudice
prevention
risk factor
safe driving
safety hazard
self-directed violence
self-esteem
self-examination
short-term consequence
solid-waste
   contamination
storage temperature
tolerance for frustration
tolerance level
weight maintenance

## Level 4

abstinence
advocacy service
alcohol dependency
antioxidant
assertive consumerism
benign
biopsy

# Health | Word List

## Level 4 (cont.)

breast examination
caffeine dependency
carcinogenic
child-care center
child abuse
cirrhosis
clinical depression
cocaine
communicable disease
conflict prevention
   strategy
consumer health service
coping strategy
date rape
dating relationship
degenerative disease
diet aid
dietary supplement
drug-related problem
drug of choice
DSS regulation
emotional health
environmental health

environmental tobacco
   smoke
EPA
fad diet
family intervention
FDA
federal agency
female sexuality
fetus
food-production control
gender differences
genetic inheritability
health-care product
health insurance
household-waste
   disposal
immune system
inhalants
interpersonal conflict
life cycle
male sexuality
malignant
marijuana
medical history
melanoma

middle age
needle sharing
nicotine
nutrition plan
OSHA
osteoporosis
paranoia
pathogen
penis
perinatal care
prenatal care
psychotherapy
refuse
regular examination
rehabilitation
reproduction
Right to Know law
sexual activity
social isolation
state agency
substance abuse
teenage pregnancy
testicle
tobacco dependency
vagina

# Physical Education | Word List

## Level 1

ability
activity
arm preparation
balance
body shape
breathing rate
catch
circling
climbing
coach
exercise
flexibility
galloping
game
game rule
glove
goal
gymnasium
headstand
heart rate
hopping
jogging
joint
jump rope
jumping
kick & strike
landing
lifting
losing
lunging
outdoor activity
overhand throw
pass a ball
perspiration
player
practice
race
ready position
riding
running
score
sit-&-reach position
skill
skipping
sliding
speed
sport
stretching
take-off
team sport
throwing
throwing arm
turn taking
turning
twisting
underhand throw
winning

## Level 2

arm & shoulder stretch
athlete
athletic equipment
balance board
baseball
basketball
basketball chest pass
bat
batting
body control
boxer
championship
competitive sport
conditioning
cool-down
course
court
curl-up
cyclist
defensive strategy
distance walk/run
diver
endurance
endurance activity
fielding
fitness level
fitness standard
follow-through
foot dribble
football
gymnastics
hand dribble
hockey
ice skates
increased heart rate
individual sport
lifestyle
lifetime sport
locomotor skill
motor skill
movement control
movement pattern
muscle soreness
muscular endurance
muscular strength
net & invasion game
nonlocomotor skill
object-control skill
offensive strategy
opponent
personal challenge
personal space
physical fitness level
physical fitness test
physical injury
power
procedure

# Physical Education | Word List

## Level 2 (cont.)

professional sport
proper nutrition
pull-up
pulse rate
punt
push-up
racing start
racket
racket sport
recovery rate
recreational league
rhythmical skill
rink
risk taking
self-assessment
self-expression through
    physical activity
serve the ball
shoot the ball
sideline
skate
skis
soccer dribble
softball
sport etiquette
sport-specific skill
sports apparatus
sports club
sportsmanship
stealing the ball
striking pattern
swimming
temporary tiredness
tennis
timed walk/run
to make a play
track
training

transition movement
traveling pattern
trunk twist
warm-up
weight-bearing activity
wheelchair sports

## Level 3

advanced movement
    skill
aerobic
aerobic capacity
anaerobic
calisthenics
cardiorespiratory
    endurance
cardiorespiratory
    exertion
dual sport
emotional health
exclusionary behavior
eye-hand coordination
fat body mass
feedback
fitness goal
freestyle swimming
frequency of training
game plan
handicapped athlete
health benefit
heart-rate recovery
heart-rate reserve
inclusive behavior
intramural sport
irregular heart rate
isometric exercise
lean body mass
leisure activity

manual dexterity
mental health
movement concept
muscle cramp
overtraining
overuse injury
psychological benefit
physiological benefit
range of motion
relaxation techniques
resistance training
resting heart rate
self-image
self-talk
spatial awareness
spike the ball
stress reduction
target heart rate
threshold
visualization
volleyball
weight control
weight training

## Level 4

abdomen
aquatics
autonomous phase of
    learning
ballistic stretching
biomechanics of
    movement
body composition
cardiovascular efficiency
center of gravity
circuit training
equilibrium
extracurricular sport

## Level 4 (cont.)

fast-twitch muscle
health-enhancing level of
    fitness
international
    competition
interval training
law of specificity

leadership role
mental imagery
overload principle
personal fitness program
physiological factor
progression principle
progressive overload
rate of perceived exertion
respiratory efficiency

reversibility
sedentary lifestyle
situational awareness
slow-twitch muscle
specificity principle
sport facility
sport psychology
static balance
static stretch

## Level 1

applause
art
artist
audience
clapping
costume
dance
entertainer
film
music
pattern
sequence
stage
theater

## Level 2

accompaniment
art form
artistic purpose
balance
beat
diction
emphasis
form
genre
improvisation
interpretation
lighting
mood
movement
originality

performance
performer
personal preference
professional
repetition
rhythm
scenery
set
setting
structure
style
subject matter
symbol
technical component
tempo
theme
timing
tone
visual artist
visual arts
work of art

## Level 3

AB form
ABA form
aesthetic criteria
aesthetics
art medium
artistic choice
audience response
aural element
body alignment
breath control

costuming
cultural context
emotional response
ensemble
expression
function of art
historical context
historical influence
historical period
kinetic element
performing arts
presentation
rehearsal
repertoire
scene
tension
texture
traditional art forms
transition
variation

## Level 4

artistic process
contemporary music
craftsmanship
emotional dimension
integration of art forms
media
technique
unity of the arts
universal concept

# Dance | Word List

## Level 1

bend
dancer
distance
ending
fall
forward
height
hop
landing
leap
middle
sideward
skip
straight
strength
stretch
turn
twist

## Level 2

balance
body position
body shape
dance phrase
dance step
energy
flexibility
focus
folk dance
following
in step
leading
line
mirroring
movement element
partner skill
personal space

rhythmic completion
shape
slide
supporting weight
taking weight
traditional dance
weight shift

## Level 3

abstracted gesture
agility
angle
articulation of
    movement
ballet
call and response
canon
chance reordering
classical dance
collapse
combination of
    movements
complementary shapes
contrasting shapes
coordination
dab
diagonal
directionality
elevation
float
glide
initiation of movement
injury-prevention
    strategy
jazz dance
level in relation to floor
movement quality
movement sequence
narrative

pantomime
punch
recovery
reordering
restructure
round
social dance
spatial pattern
square dance
sustain
swing
tap dance
theatrical dance
vibratory
warm-up technique

## Level 4

abstract dance
alignment
axial movement
Balinese dance
base of support
bharata natyam dance
body-part articulation
body image
central initiation
choreographic
choreographic process
choreographic structure
distal initiation
dynamic qualities or
    efforts
Ghanaian dance
Noh dance
kinesphere
kinesthetic awareness
line of gravity
locomotor movement

# Dance | Word List

**Level 4 (cont.)**

Middle Eastern dance
modern dance
movement elevation
movement phrase
movement theme

musicality
nonlocomotor
   movement
palindrome
penultimate movement
percussive
projection

rhythmic acuity
rondo
skeletal alignment
tempi
theme and variation
time element

# Music | Word List

## Level 1

body sound
instrument
loudness
lullaby
melody
musician
partner song
piano
sing
song
strum
swaying
symbol for note
voice

## Level 2

accent
alto
arrangement
art song
band instrument
bass
chord
classroom instruments
compose
composer
conductor
cue
diminuendo
Dixieland music
dotted note
drum machine
duet
echo
eighth note
electronic instrument
electronic sound

elements of music
embellishment
flat
folk
forte
fretted instrument
gospel music
guitar
half note
harmony
key signature
keyboard
keyboard instruments
legato
levels of difficulty
major key
march
measure
MIDI
minor key
Musical Instrument
    Digital Interface
musical phrase
musical piece
musical staff
nontraditional sound
notation
orchestra conductor
orchestral instrument
patriotic song
percussion instrument
pitch
posture
progression
quarter note
recorder
repeat
rest
rhythmic variation
ritard

rock music
round
scale
sequencer
sharp
sixteenth note
skipping
snapping
soprano
staccato
staff
standard notation
string instrument
symbol for articulation
synthesizer
tenor
tie
time signature
traditional sound
treble clef
ukulele
whole note
work song

## Level 3

a capella
articulation
barbershop quartet
bass clef
blues
bow control
chorded zithers
chorus
classical
coda
composition
crescendo
dynamic change

# Music | Word List

## Level 3 (cont.)

dynamic level
harmonic
    accompaniment
harmonic instrument
hymn
instrumental literature
interval
intonation
jazz
jingle
level-1 difficulty
level-2 difficulty
level-3 difficulty
level-4 difficulty
level-5 difficulty
madrigal
mallet instruments
marcato
melodic embellishment
melodic instrument
melodic line
melodic ostinato
melodic phrase
meter
meter change
meter signature
music in four parts
music in two and three
    parts
oboe

opera
phrasing
pitch notation
playing by ear
playing position
pop
presto
quartet
range
recorder-type
    instruments
refrain
release
rhythmic ostinato
sight read
sonata
stick control
suite
sympathy
symphonic
syncopation
timbre
tonality
traditional sound source
trio
triple meter
wind instrument

## Level 4

accelerando
acoustic instrument

alla breve
allegro
andante
Broadway musical
chord progression
compositional device
compositional technique
consonance
contour
decrescendo
dissonance
duple meter
expressive device
instrumental score
instrumentation
inversion
oratorio
ostinato
pentatonic melody
pentatonic tonality
point of climax
register
retrograde
rhythmic phrase
rubato
staves
swing
tempo marking
vocal literature
vocal score

# Theater | Word List

## Level 1

act
actor
dramatic play
story
writer

## Level 2

acting skill
action
cast
character
classroom dramatization
dialogue
drama
line
makeup
production
prop
role
social pretend play
villain

## Level 3

archetype
atmosphere
avocation
character motivation
characterization
classical
constructed meaning
direction
director
dramatic media
dramatization
electronic media
empathy
formal production
informal production
locale
new art forms
nonlocomotor
    movement
oral element
physical environment
pitch
playwright
production value
publicity
script
sensory recall
set design
staging
study guide
superhero
suspense
theater literacy
trickster
visual element
vocal pitch

## Level 4

acting method
aesthetic achievement
American theater
dramatic text
heritage
musical theater
oral symbol
physical & chemical
    properties of lighting,
    color, electricity
production requirement
promotional plan
stage management
unified production
    concept
visual symbol

# Visual Arts | Word List

**Level 1**

brush
camera
paint

**Level 2**

art material
art process
art technique
art tools
artwork
balance
canvas
cardboard
casting
clay
color
color variation
complementary color
composition
construction
contrast
cool color
depth
elicited response
knife
medium

metal
models
oil paint
overlapping
perspective
plastic
scissors
sculpture
shading
shape
size variation
stone
varying color
varying size
videotape
viewer
visual structure
warm color
watercolor
wood

**Level 3**

art elements
art history
brayers
contemporary meaning
definition
design element

easel
expressive features
form
hue
intensity
kiln
laser
lathe
line
motion
placement
press
space
spatial characteristic
temporal structure
texture
value
visual concept

**Level 4**

art criticism
art object
halftone
highlight
negative space
organizational principle
positive space
shadow edge

## Level 1

backspace key
computer
computer program
diskette
enter key
escape key
floppy disk
hand position
home row
Internet
keyboard
login
menu
monitor
mouse
power-up
power supply
printer
reboot
return key
space bar
special keys
World Wide Web

## Level 2

alphanumeric keys
back-up
connecting cable
copy
copyright law
cursor
data
data deletion
data records
data retrieval

data storage
database
delete key
desktop
disk drive
download
e-mail
edit
electronic form
file folder
function keys
graphics
hard disk
hard drive
hardware
help system
home page
information exchange
information retrieval
Internet browser
load a program
memory
modem
multiple solutions
online
print form
software
software piracy
speed of communication
storage
storage device
stored data
technical difficulty
troubleshooting
upload
virus
word processor

## Level 3

automated machine
bulletin board system
capacity
CD-ROM
central processing unit
computer fraud
computer hacking
copyright violation
data access
data display
data processing
data update
decoder
designed object
desktop publishing
    software
digitized
disassembly
document formatting
e-learning
feedback
file management
format
formatting
function
human-operated
    machine
icon
input device
Internet Service Provider
Intranet
invasion of privacy
local network system
malfunction
man-made object
misconnected

## Level 3 (cont.)

mismatched
navigation (Internet)
network
nonphysical object
output
output device
programming command
programming language
record management
search techniques
sort techniques
special purpose program
specialized machine
spreadsheet
steps in the design
　　process
system failure
tape drive
text format
touch screen
URL
virus setting
voice recorder

## Level 4

artifact
batch production
binary
biotechnology
bit
Boolean search
byte
chat room

chip
closed-loop system
coordinated subsystems
CPU
debug
dedicated line
design principle
dual effect
e-paper
encoder
export a file
external storage
feedback system
field
frame
gigabyte
hardware limitations
hardware platform
hardware trade-off
HTML
import a file
information transfer
initialize
intelligent system
iterative process
kilobyte
linear system
listserv
machine-to-machine
macro
magnetic field
mail merge
mathematical modeling
megabyte
merge files
microprocessor

modified design
natural object
open-loop system
operating system
optimized solution
overdesign
patent
performance testing
peripheral device
person-to-machine
person-to-person
pixel
RAM
rate of diffusion
recursive process
redundancy
repetitive process
scanner
service provider
simple system
simulation
software application
sound recorder
spam
story board
streaming
subsystem
system design
systems thinking
telecommunications
telecomputing
template
transmitter
usenet newsreader
Web ring

# Related ASCD Resources

For pricing and other information, or to order these materials, visit ASCD's Online Store at http://shop.ascd.org. Or call 1-800-933-2723.

## Building Academic Vocabulary: Student Notebook

*By Robert J. Marzano and Debra J. Pickering*

Students use the colorful worksheets in these vocabulary notebooks to record their vocabulary terms and develop their deep understanding of each term. Each page in the notebook takes students through a research-based instructional approach. Throughout the school year, students add new information about their terms as their understanding of the terms deepens and matures. A single set provides five students in any grade level with classroom materials they use all year long to build their academic vocabulary.

Notebook Materials (Stock #105154): $48.95 (ASCD members and nonmembers).
  Note: Each set includes materials for five students.
Binders (Stock #105173): $4.00 each (ASCD members and nonmembers).
  Note: Each binder holds one student's notebook materials.

### Bonus for Systemwide Adoption: Building Academic Vocabulary Web Site
With a purchase of 20 or more sets of student notebook materials, get free access to a special Building Academic Vocabulary Web site for word selection. The site allows groups of educators in a school, district, or state to select the words they believe are the most important for their students to learn. It contains the vocabulary lists in all content areas and grade levels and provides a process for prioritizing the words. Users of the site will be able to download their prioritized list to distribute to all teachers using the Building Academic Vocabulary program. Call 1-800-933-2723, ext. 5634, for details on adopting this program in your school, district, or state.

## The Six-Step Process for Teaching Vocabulary Video

Here's the best new tool to show that effective vocabulary instruction is about concept development instead of just giving students a word list. Use the videos or DVD with teacher groups and workshops to explain why it's easier for students to understand academic content when they've been taught the academic terms in your content standards. Then use classroom scenes to introduce teachers to the most effective way for teaching academic vocabulary.

Demonstrations from elementary and secondary classrooms show examples of a research-based, six-step vocabulary teaching process as actual classroom teachers use the ASCD student and teacher materials to build students' academic vocabulary. These classroom examples and lots of teacher tips ensure that teachers grasp the instructional process right away and find it easier to implement. When all the teachers in your school focus on the same academic vocabulary and teach it in the same way, your school has a powerful comprehensive approach for building student knowledge and understanding in the content areas.

Set of two 30-minute videotapes, one in an elementary setting and one in a secondary setting (Stock #405169) or a DVD with both elementary and secondary programs (Stock #605169): $123 (ASCD members); $165 (nonmembers).

Individual Tapes:
Tape 1: A Six-Step Process for Teaching Vocabulary—Elementary (Stock #405170)
Tape 2: A Six-Step Process for Teaching Vocabulary—Secondary (Stock #405171)
Price per tape: $89 (ASCD members); $119 (nonmembers).

## Building Background Knowledge for Academic Achievement: Research on What Works in Schools

*By Robert J. Marzano*

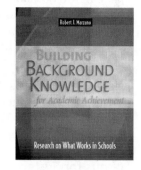

Go back to the beginning with this book to learn why insufficient background knowledge is a cause of chronic low achievement. Then discover how a carefully structured combination of vocabulary instruction and sustained silent reading can rescue low achievers and boost the academic performance of all students. Drawing from 35 years of research, Robert J. Marzano uses detailed vignettes to provide you with the tools you need to close achievement gaps.

Stock #104017; $21.95 (ASCD members); $26.95 (nonmembers).

## Building Academic Background Knowledge

Use this video series (available on tape or DVD) and facilitator's guide with teacher teams and other school groups to explain why direct teaching of certain vocabulary terms leads to higher academic achievement. Research expert Robert J. Marzano explains the importance of teaching content-area vocabulary terms to all learners, especially for low-achieving students who tend not to have been exposed to academic vocabulary necessary for school success. Classroom scenes from a variety of subject areas and grade levels illustrate how to build students' background knowledge and help them overcome obstacles to learning. Interviews with cognitive neuroscientists and teaching experts show how these strategies relate to how the brain naturally learns. Workshop outlines and learning activities in the accompanying facilitator's guide get everyone in your school focused on implementing practices that research shows result in greater student achievement.

Entire video series on three 30-minute tapes (Stock #405020) or on one DVD (Stock #605024) plus a facilitator's guide: $445 (ASCD members); $545 (nonmembers).

Individual Tapes:
Tape 1: The Art and Science of Teaching (Stock #405021)
Tape 2: Teaching Vocabulary, Characteristics 1–3 (Stock #405022)
Tape 3: Teaching Vocabulary, Characteristics 4–7 (Stock #405023)
Price per tape: $189 (ASCD members); $229 (nonmembers)

# About ASCD

Founded in 1943, the Association for Supervision and Curriculum Development is a nonpartisan, nonprofit education association, with headquarters in Alexandria, Virginia, USA. ASCD's mission statement: *ASCD, a community of educators, advocating sound policies and sharing best practices to achieve the success of each learner.* Membership in ASCD includes a subscription to the award-winning journal *Educational Leadership*, the newsletter *Education Update*, and other products and services. ASCD sponsors affiliate organizations around the world; participates in collaborations and networks; holds conferences, institutes, and training programs; produces publications in a variety of media; sponsors recognition and awards programs; and provides research information on education issues.

   ASCD provides many services to educators—prekindergarten through grade 12—as well as to others in the education community, including parents, school board members, administrators, and university professors and students. For further information, contact ASCD via telephone: 1-800-933-2723 or 1-703-578-9600; fax: 1-703-575-5400; or e-mail: member@ascd.org. Or write to ASCD, Information Services, 1703 N. Beauregard St., Alexandria, VA 22311-1714 USA. You can find ASCD on the World Wide Web at www.ascd.org.
ASCD's Executive Director is Gene R. Carter.

## 2005–06 Board of Directors

Mary Ellen Freeley *(President)*, Richard Hanzelka *(President-Elect)*, Martha Bruckner *(Immediate Past President)*, Donald Davis, Lavinia T. Dickerson, Margaret S. Edwards, Debra A. Hill, Linda Mariotti, Doris Matthews, Anthony Mello, Michaelene Meyer, Gail Elizabeth Pope, Keith Rohwer, Thelma L. Spencer, Sandra Stoddard, Valerie Truesdale

## Belief Statements

Fundamental to ASCD is our concern for people, both individually and collectively.
- We believe that the individual has intrinsic worth.
- We believe that all people have the ability and the need to learn.
- We believe that all children have a right to safety, love, and learning.
- We believe that a high-quality, public system of education open to all is imperative for society to flourish.
- We believe that diversity strengthens society and should be honored and protected.
- We believe that broad, informed participation committed to a common good is critical to democracy.
- We believe that humanity prospers when people work together.
- ASCD also recognizes the potential and power of a healthy organization.
- We believe that healthy organizations purposefully provide for self-renewal.
- We believe that the culture of an organization is a major factor shaping individual attitudes and behaviors.
- We believe that shared values and common goals shape and change the culture of healthy organizations.